Eyewitness
CITY

New York City
souvenir

Becak cycle rickshaw,
Yogyakarta

Venice festival
mask

Bronze sculpture of Romulus
and Remus with the wolf, Rome

Akbil transit
passes, Istanbul

Poker
chips

12th-century
trebuchet

Ancient Mayan
ball player

Eyewitness
CITY

Italian mayor's sash

Written by
PHILIP STEELE

Street signs,
New York City

DK Publishing

DK

LONDON, NEW YORK,
MELBOURNE, MUNICH, AND DELHI

Consultant Max Steuer

DK DELHI
Project editor Ankush Saikia
Project designer Govind Mittal
Editor Pieu Biswas
Designer Prashant Kumar
DTP designers Tarun Sharma, Jagtar Singh
Editorial manager Suchismita Banerjee
Design manager Romi Chakraborty
Production manager Pankaj Sharma
Head of publishing Aparna Sharma

DK LONDON
Senior editor Rob Houston
Editor Jessamy Wood
Managing editor Julie Ferris
Managing art editor Owen Peyton Jones
Associate publisher Andrew Macintyre
Picture researcher Ria Jones
Production editor Marc Staples
Production controller Charlotte Oliver
Jacket designer Smiljka Surla
US editor Margaret Parrish

First published in the United States in 2011
by DK Publishing, 375 Hudson Street, New York, New York 10014
Copyright © 2011 Dorling Kindersley Limited, London

11 12 13 14 15 10 9 8 7 6 5 4 3 2 1
175393—03/11

A catalog record for this book is available
from the Library of Congress.
ISBN: 978-0-7566-7207-2 (Hardcover)
978-0-7566-7208-9 (Library binding)

Color reproduction by MDP, UK
Printed and bound by
Toppan Printing Co. (Shenzhen) Ltd., China

www.dk.com

Swiss guard
in Vatican City

Tiwanaku flask

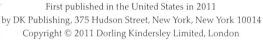

Chinese lantern,
symbol of
Chinatown

Colored diamonds,
Johannesburg, South Africa

Nissan PIVO 2,
electric concept car

Skyscrapers,
New York City

Contents

Jeepney, Manila, Philippines

What is a city?

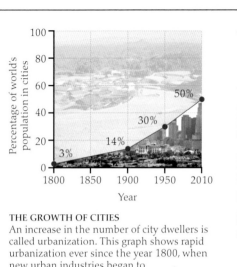

HALF OF THE WORLD'S POPULATION of 7 billion people now live in urban areas—towns and cities—rather than in the countryside. The rapid growth of cities is set to continue. Towns with large populations are generally called cities, but the exact definition of the word "city" varies from one country to another. The word can describe smaller urban areas that are centers of regional government, law, or religion. In some countries, "city" describes only the inner districts of a large urban area. Big cities are places to meet, do business, exchange ideas, study, and have fun. Though they can sometimes be lonely places, throughout history cities have led the advance in art, politics, business, and other aspects of human civilization.

THE GROWTH OF CITIES
An increase in the number of city dwellers is called urbanization. This graph shows rapid urbanization ever since the year 1800, when new urban industries began to offer working opportunities for country people. People are still moving into cities in search of higher incomes and better services.

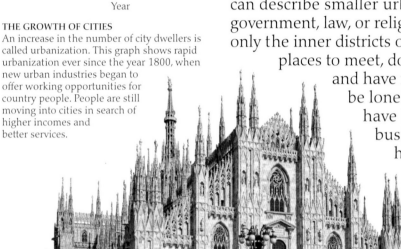

A CATHEDRAL CITY
In medieval Europe, a city was any town that had a cathedral, the chief Christian church of the region. Cities competed to build the largest and most splendid cathedrals, not only to demonstrate their faith in God, but also to show off their prosperity. This cathedral in Milan, Italy, was built between 1386 and 1965. It is the fourth-largest church in the world. Cathedrals today are not only centers of religion, but also a record of a city's history over the centuries.

URBAN GIANTS
China has a tradition of city building dating back thousands of years. In the 21st century, the country is going through a new phase of urbanization, with skyscrapers springing up like mushrooms. This is the Pudong development zone in the eastern port of Shanghai, a city that is the biggest commercial and financial center in the world's fastest-growing economy. Shanghai currently has a population of more than 18 million.

CENTERS OF GOVERNMENT
Switzerland's National Council meets in the parliament buildings of the federal capital, the beautiful old city of Bern. Cities have often served as regional or national centers of power. They may be the headquarters of royal courts, assemblies, and governments, as well as centers of law and order. Many city workers may be employed as administrators (civil servants).

VIVID SYDNEY
Projected lights and artworks on its roof turn the Sydney Opera House into an electric canvas. This Australian city's Festival of Light, Music, and Ideas is promoted as "Vivid Sydney." For nearly a month, performances, exhibitions, and debates highlight the city's position as a creative hub in the Asia–Pacific region. More than 200,000 people attended the festival in 2009. Cities have always been centers of cultural activity, where branches of the arts such as drama, opera, sculpture, and architecture all had their origins. Arts festivals make cities exciting places to live in and attract many visitors.

CITIES GO TO WORK
The year is 1867 and in France a massive steam hammer is being used to forge iron. The heavy industries that encouraged urbanization in the 19th century literally shaped the new cities. Iron was used to build railroads and stations, bridges, towers, and viaducts. The cities of this age were crowded, noisy, and sooty. Work was hard and poorly paid, but as ever, it was the chief reason for a city's existence.

CITY AND COUNTRY
About 2,600 years ago, a Greek writer of fables called Aesop was already pointing out the differences between urban and rural ways of life. In his tale of a country mouse who visits the town, Aesop portrayed rural life as poor and simple, but honest. This was in contrast to city life, which was wealthy and comfortable, but full of danger, deception, and worries. This story has been retold by many children's writers, including Beatrix Potter in 1917.

The first towns

EARLY HUMANS ROAMED from one place to another. They survived by hunting wild animals and gathering plants. It was about 12,000 years ago, in western Asia, that people learned to grow crops and herd animals. This change meant that humans could control their own food supplies, allowing permanent settled communities. Over time, some small farming villages grew into towns that served as local trading centers. Complex social structures, legal systems, religions, and written scripts developed in the towns. From 4000 BCE, some urban areas had grown to such an extent that they dwarfed nearby towns. These were the first cities.

FARMERS FEED CITIES
Farming in China began around 6000 BCE. As in other parts of the world, the controlled supply of food that resulted from the invention of agriculture meant villages and towns could be settled. These lush green terraced fields in Guangxi Province in southern China supply agricultural produce to nearby modern-day cities.

LIVING TOGETHER
Archeological excavations at Çatalhöyük in southern Turkey offer an amazing glimpse of urban life nearly 10,000 years ago. Simple plastered mud-brick houses were clustered together with no streets between them. The 10,000 residents accessed their houses via wooden ladders on the roofs. They lived by hunting, farming, and trading. They also made pottery, jewelry, and textiles. Their religious shrines were decorated with bulls' horns.

GREEK CITY-STATE
Athens, the capital of Greece, today has a population of more than 3 million. About 2,500 years ago, it was home to almost 60,000 people. Athens grew from a small independent community into a powerful city-state (a city that ruled the surrounding region). Like many ancient cities, Athens was built on high ground (around a rock called the Acropolis) and surrounded by walls for added defense.

One of the 46 outer pillars of the temple

The Parthenon, temple of the ancient Greek goddess Athena, at the Acropolis, or citadel, in Athens

Flat roof built of oak timbers, reeds, and mud

Sheep figure carved from bone

OLDEST WALLED CITY

This little animal figure, made of bone, was found by archeologists at Hamoukar in Syria. This site dates back to around 4000 BCE, making it perhaps the oldest walled city ever discovered. It housed about 25,000 people. Cooking pots, bread ovens, wells, and seals for making marks on clay tablets have been discovered at Hamoukar. The city was destroyed by warfare around 3500 BCE.

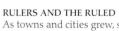

Mayan king

RULERS AND THE RULED

As towns and cities grew, society became more complex. This pyramid shows the social structure in a typical Mayan city, such as Bonampak (in what is now Guatemala) in about 790 CE. At the top was a king, followed by nobles and priests. The production of pottery, metalwork, and tools gave work to other social groups, such as craftsmen. At the lowest level were the farmers, laborers, and slaves who helped to feed, build, and maintain the cities.

Members of the royal family

Nobles, priests, and warriors

Merchants, officials, and craftsmen

Farmers, laborers, and slaves

HUBS OF TRADE

From early times, cities became centers for making pottery, textiles, jewelry, and weapons. These could be traded far and wide. Trading links helped cities become wealthy and build powerful empires. Between 600 and 800 CE, the cities of Tiwanaku and Wari in the Andes mountains of South America traded in textiles and fine pottery. Merchants from Tiwanaku used llamas to carry goods to other towns and regions.

Tiwanaku flask

CITY BUSINESS

To run a city, people needed ways of writing and counting. This clay tablet is marked with little wedge-shaped symbols called cuneiform script. The tablet dates back to 2031 BCE and lists the labor and wages required to plow fields in the city of Umma, the ruins of which are located in present-day Iraq. Scripts like this allowed people to send messages, write down laws, and keep records of taxes paid. Thousands of such written tablets could be stored in palace archives.

Clay tablet from the ancient Sumerian city of Umma

Bronze sculpture of Romulus and Remus with the wolf

FOUNDING MYTHS

The great city of Rome grew from a group of villages in the Tiber Valley in Italy. The people of Rome had several stories about the origin of their city. According to one, Rome was founded in 753 BCE by Romulus, the son of Mars, who was the Roman god of war. Romulus and his twin brother Remus were abandoned as babies, but a wolf raised them on the site of the future city. This tale was still famous in the city some 2,000 years later, when a bronze sculpture of the wolf and the twins was cast.

Where and why?

FOR CITIES TO DEVELOP AND PROSPER, they need to be sited where people have access to fresh water, food, and building materials. Ideal locations range from hilltops that are easily defended, to valleys offering protection from the weather. Cities are often built where there are natural resources such as fuel or diamonds that can be mined and traded. Many cities were founded at places where roads and trading routes intersected, or along rivers or the coast from where goods could be transported. These cities developed over time and grew into hubs of industry and trade. A capital city is officially the chief city of a nation, state, or region. It is usually the center of government, though it may not be the biggest or busiest city.

THE RIVER AS LIFELINE

Cities are built near rivers as these provide water for drinking, and for irrigating crops. Rivers are also used to transport people and goods. The Arno River flows through Florence, Italy, in the fertile Arno Valley. Florence was renowned for its textiles, especially wool, and the river provided a trading route. Over the ages, these advantages helped the city develop as a center of business, science, and art. However, the river sometimes causes problems by flooding the city.

Lincoln Memorial on a US one-cent coin, or penny

UNITED STATES of AMERICA
E·PLURIBUS·UNUM·
ONE CENT

CAPITAL CITY

Washington, D.C., the capital of the United States, was founded in 1790 as the center of government for the newly independent nation. D.C. stands for District of Columbia, a special territory set aside by law from the 50 states of the US as the permanent national capital. Washington's public monuments, such as the Lincoln Memorial, were built in the styles of ancient Greece and Rome, as these civilizations had inspired the founders of the new nation. The Lincoln Memorial was built as a tribute to Abraham Lincoln (1809–1865), the 16th president of the US.

TRADE LINKS

More than 2,000 years ago, a network of trading routes called the Silk Road stretched from China to western Asia and Europe. Traders carried silk, tea, spices, and other precious items along these routes, relaying them from town to town. These towns developed bustling markets where the traders could buy and sell their goods. Some of these towns grew into wealthy cities, especially those sited at junctions where different arms of the trading route came together, such as Samarkand in Uzbekistan, which marked the halfway point on the Silk Road.

The German city of Bremen, on the Weser River, was a great center of trade in the Middle Ages. In the 1800s, the river began to silt up, so large ships could no longer reach the city. A new deep-water port called Bremerhaven was built 37 miles (60 km) downstream, where the river enters the North Sea, and a town quickly grew up around it. By the 1850s, there was so much trade passing through and so many people boarding ships from here to emigrate to North America, that Bremerhaven had become a thriving city. Today, Bremerhaven's main industry is still the port, which handles thousands of container ships every year.

Tower crane used in skyscraper construction

DIAMOND RUSH
The discovery of valuable mineral resources such as diamonds or gold can lead to the sudden growth of new cities, often in remote regions. Prospectors, miners, and suppliers come to seek their fortune, opening up opportunities for other people. The city of Kimberley in South Africa grew up around diamond mines in the 1860s and 1870s.

BUILT FROM SCRATCH
Sometimes it is easier to build a new city than to develop an existing one. Shenzhen was a fishing village in the delta region of the Pearl River, in southern China. In 1979, the government chose this area just north of Hong Kong for an experiment to attract international investment, creating a special economic zone with a brand-new city at its heart. Tower cranes rapidly created forests of skyscrapers. Today, Shenzhen is a booming center of business, finance, and industry, with a busy port that has easy access to the South China Sea. More than 8 million people have come from all over China to settle in or around the city in search of work.

Camels carry goods through the Hindu Kush mountains in Afghanistan, once part of the Silk Road

Spires and domes

NOT ALL OF THE WORLD'S great cities came into being because of trade, politics, or a favorable location. There are also cities of ideas, with ancient universities and libraries that are known for their education and learning. Such cities have attracted thinkers and students for hundreds of years. Cities can also be centers of religious belief, where people come to worship and pray. From the Middle Ages onward, the Christian cities of Europe raised massive stone cathedrals with tall, pointed pinnacles called spires. Some of these were built over periods of hundreds of years. In other parts of the medieval world people were building temples, mosques, synagogues, and other religious monuments. Some holy cities attract pilgrims—travelers who make a journey to pray at a particular sacred site.

Ceremonial halberd

Swiss Guard in Vatican City

VATICAN CITY
This independent city-state is the world's smallest nation. It is located entirely within Rome, the Italian capital, and has a population of only 800. Vatican City is the headquarters of the Roman Catholic branch of the Christian faith, and includes a vast church called St. Peter's Basilica.

TO MECCA
Hajj, or pilgrimage, is a basic duty for all Muslims. Every year the city of Mecca, the birthplace of the prophet Muhammad, is visited by up to 2.5 million pilgrims from all over the world. They walk seven times around the Ka'aba, the most sacred site of Islam. Mecca, which is in Saudi Arabia, has grown into a large city as a result of the Hajj. Today, it is home to about 1.7 million people. Non-Muslims are not allowed to enter the city.

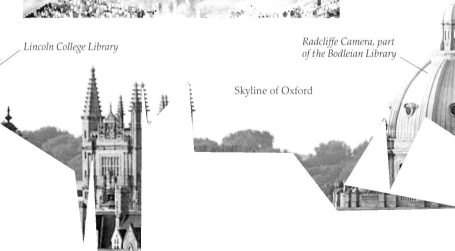

Lincoln College Library

Skyline of Oxford

Radcliffe Camera, part of the Bodleian Library

CITY OF THE SIKHS
A Sikh bathes in the sacred pool in front of the magnificent Harmandir Sahib, or Golden Temple, at Amritsar. Founded in the Punjab region of India in 1574, Amritsar is a holy city for all followers of the Sikh religion. The city gets its name from the pool, known as the Amrit Sarovar. Sikhs make up about three-quarters of the city's 1.5 million citizens. The community kitchen at the Golden Temple provides free food to up to 10,000 pilgrims every day.

Manuscript from Timbuktu

ANCIENT LIBRARIES
Religious beliefs often traveled along trading routes, carried by merchants from one city to another. Where religious faith took root, learning often followed. The city of Timbuktu, in Mali, Africa, was founded in the Middle Ages. Its merchants traded across the Sahara desert, carrying salt, gold, ivory, slaves—and the Islamic faith. The mud-brick-built city soon had mosques, a university, and many libraries. The Ahmed Baba Institute in the city preserves a collection of some 30,000 manuscripts.

PRAYING IN JERUSALEM
The ancient city of Jerusalem is considered holy by three faiths—Judaism, Christianity, and Islam. Many Jews visit the city to pray at the Western Wall (left), part of the temple built by Herod the Great in about 19 BCE and destroyed by the Romans in 70 CE. Muslims pray here, too, at the al-Aqsa mosque. The gleaming Dome of the Rock (background) is a shrine completed in 692 CE and is the world's oldest surviving Islamic building. For Christians, one of the most holy pilgrimage sites in Jerusalem is the Church of the Holy Sepulcher.

DREAMING SPIRES
The city of Oxford, England, has been one of the world's great centers of study and research for more than 900 years. The University of Oxford is today made up of 38 colleges. Over the centuries, museums, theaters, libraries, and churches were built here because of the university. The poet Matthew Arnold called Oxford the "city of dreaming spires," a romantic description of its architecture. Oxford also has separate commercial and industrial districts.

Christchurch College

Church of St. Mary's

All Souls College

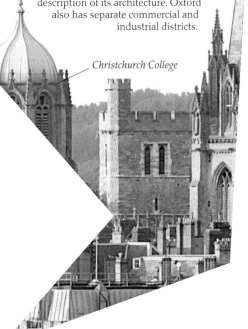

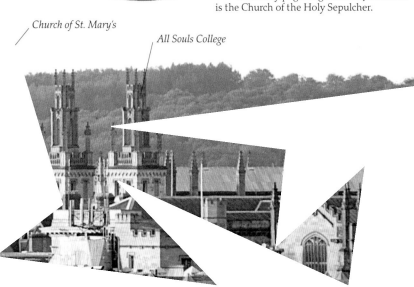

Eternal cities

WHILE SOME CITIES FALL into decline and are abandoned, the world's longest-lasting cities have been inhabited successfully for thousands of years. Rome, the capital of Italy, is often called the "eternal city." Ancient Romans believed that the city would last forever, and Rome is still thriving today, with a population of nearly 3 million. Cities like Rome survive by changing and developing over time. New rulers invade and conquer, bringing new religions and customs. As the centuries pass, cities that grew up along trade routes adapt to the new people and goods that travel through. Many enduring cities are centers of faith and the visiting pilgrims ensure the cities' continued survival.

FOREVER ROME
Rome was the powerful capital of the Roman Empire, a civilization that stretched across much of Europe for hundreds of years. The empire eventually collapsed, but as Christianity spread, Rome became the center of the Roman Catholic Church. Rome's best-preserved old building, the Pantheon, was originally built as a temple to ancient pagan gods and, like Rome, has changed hands many times. The Roman emperor Hadrian rebuilt it in 125 CE after a fire, and Pope Boniface VIII turned it into a Christian church in 609 CE.

Cowrie shell from the Red Sea

FACE OF THE PAST
Jericho, a city in Palestine in the Middle East, has been invaded and conquered throughout its history by many different rulers, including Assyrians, Jews, Persians, Greeks, and Arabs. Jericho is one of the world's earliest settlements that is still inhabited today—people first lived at this site in the valley of the Jordan River more than 11,000 years ago. This skull, plastered and painted to resemble the person when alive, dates back to before 7000 BCE.

Plastered skull from ancient Jericho

TEA TO SEAL A DEAL
Traders often offer a glass of black tea from these splendid urns to customers as they haggle over the prices of textiles or antiques at the market, or souk, in Damascus, the capital of Syria. A vast, ancient network of trade routes, known as the Silk Road (see page 10), came together at Damascus, and buying and selling has been at the center of city life ever since. Damascus was known to the ancient Egyptians as early as 1400 BCE, and it became an Islamic capital in around 600 CE. Of all the modern capital cities, Damascus has had the longest continuous settlement—people have lived here for at least 11,000 years.

Tea seller in Damascus

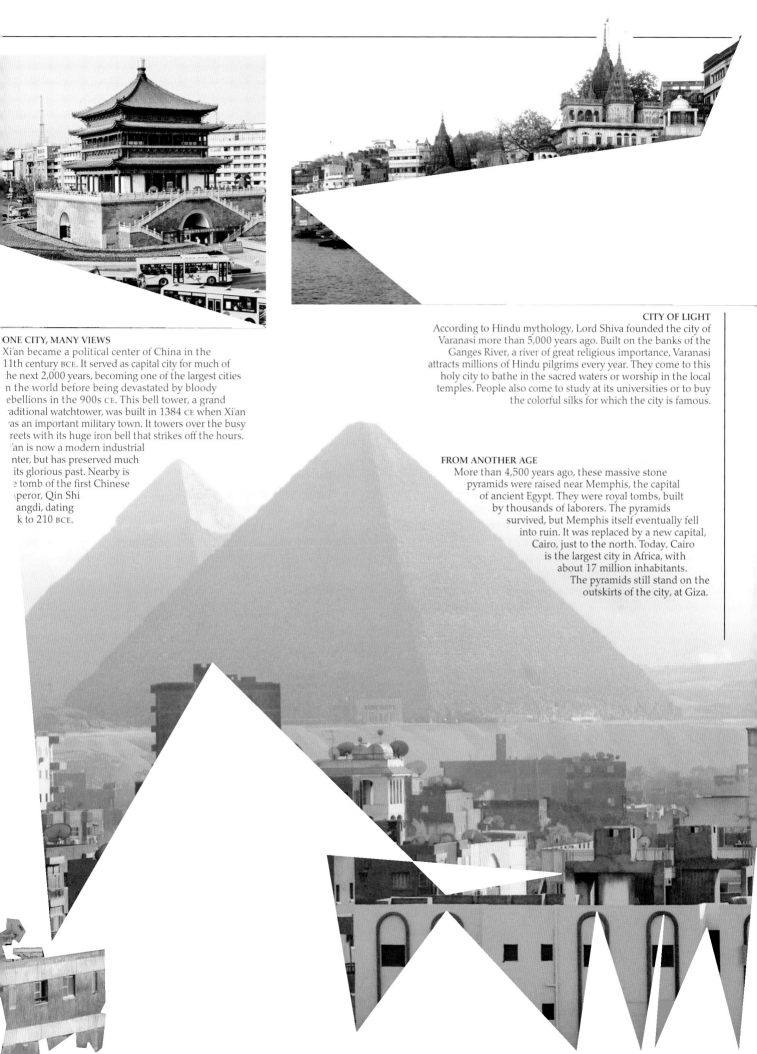

ONE CITY, MANY VIEWS

Xi'an became a political center of China in the 11th century BCE. It served as capital city for much of the next 2,000 years, becoming one of the largest cities in the world before being devastated by bloody rebellions in the 900s CE. This bell tower, a grand traditional watchtower, was built in 1384 CE when Xi'an was an important military town. It towers over the busy streets with its huge iron bell that strikes off the hours. Xi'an is now a modern industrial center, but has preserved much of its glorious past. Nearby is the tomb of the first Chinese emperor, Qin Shi Huangdi, dating back to 210 BCE.

CITY OF LIGHT

According to Hindu mythology, Lord Shiva founded the city of Varanasi more than 5,000 years ago. Built on the banks of the Ganges River, a river of great religious importance, Varanasi attracts millions of Hindu pilgrims every year. They come to this holy city to bathe in the sacred waters or worship in the local temples. People also come to study at its universities or to buy the colorful silks for which the city is famous.

FROM ANOTHER AGE

More than 4,500 years ago, these massive stone pyramids were raised near Memphis, the capital of ancient Egypt. They were royal tombs, built by thousands of laborers. The pyramids survived, but Memphis itself eventually fell into ruin. It was replaced by a new capital, Cairo, just to the north. Today, Cairo is the largest city in Africa, with about 17 million inhabitants. The pyramids still stand on the outskirts of the city, at Giza.

Forgotten cities

SOME CITIES SEEM TO HAVE EXISTED forever, while others have disappeared off the map. Once powerful and famous, they may fall into ruin and be forgotten by all, except a few local people. The location of some cities may be lost altogether, as buildings are buried under sand or overgrown by jungle. Cities may be completely destroyed by earthquakes or volcanoes, by warfare, or by fire. Others may have to be abandoned due to changes in climate that cause droughts or floods. A river may alter its course, or a port may get silted up and become unusable. The search for lost cities presents an exciting challenge for explorers, archeologists, and historians.

THE ROSE-RED CITY
The ancient city of Petra, now in Jordan, was carved out of cliffs of red sandstone. From 312 BCE, it was the capital of the Nabataean kingdom and was later ruled by the Romans. Petra relied on the spice trade across the Arabian desert, but that declined when more goods were transported by sea. Shaken by a series of earthquakes, much of the city was ruined and buried under sand. The world came to know about Petra when Johann Ludwig Burckhardt, a Swiss explorer, rediscovered it in 1812.

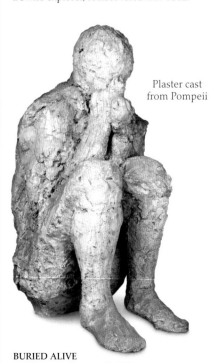

Plaster cast from Pompeii

DREAMS TURN TO ASHES
King Darius I of Persia (modern-day Iran) ruled a vast empire that stretched from Egypt to India. Around 515 BCE, Darius's son Xerxes the Great built a new capital city called Persepolis, or Parsa. The city had grand palaces, halls, and treasuries. These are the ruins of the council hall at Persepolis, and they show a procession of representatives of conquered nations. The city was captured and looted by the invading army of Alexander the Great in 330 BCE and then destroyed by fire.

1931 poster advertising adventurous guided tours to Angkor

Relief sculpture of official carrying gifts for the king

ROOTED IN HISTORY
In 1860, French naturalist Henri Mouhot visited Angkor in Cambodia. He was fascinated by its great stone buildings hidden beneath creepers and roots. Angkor dates back to the Khmer Empire of the 1100s. It had been at the center of an urban area of more than 155 sq miles (400 sq km), which included several smaller towns and countless temples. Angkor Wat (the "city temple") is one of the most impressive religious sites in the world.

BURIED ALIVE
In 79 CE, a volcano called Vesuvius (see page 60) erupted in Italy, burying the city of Pompeii under ash. Thousands of people choked to death. Only in the 1700s did treasure hunters and archeologists start to excavate the site. They discovered hollow spaces formed in the compressed ash after the decay of people's bodies. More than a century later, people found that by filling these hollows with plaster they could recreate the shapes of those who had died.

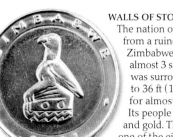

WALLS OF STONES
The nation of Zimbabwe takes its name from a ruined African city called Great Zimbabwe. This royal city covered almost 3 sq miles (7.5 sq km), and was surrounded by granite walls up to 36 ft (11 m) high. It was occupied for almost 300 years from 1270. Its people traded in cattle, ivory, and gold. This modern coin shows one of the eight stone-carved birds discovered at the site.

FUTURE NIGHTMARE
Could changes to Earth's climate reduce today's great cities to ruins? This scene from the 2004 science fiction film *The Day after Tomorrow* imagines New York City in the grip of a new ice age. The film also shows Los Angeles being destroyed by tornadoes, Tokyo devastated by hailstorms, and New Delhi buried under snow. The idea is exaggerated, but it is interesting to think what our own cities would look like to archeologists in the future.

AFTER THE BLAST
This satellite image shows the Greek islands of Santorini in the Aegean Sea. These were once parts of a single island, but a volcanic eruption more than 3,500 years ago blasted its center apart. Excavations in Thera, the largest of the existing islands, have revealed part of an ancient trading city with streets, piped water, and fine wall paintings.

Walls and towers

THE FIRST CITIES were surrounded by high walls and towers. They helped protect the inhabitants from enemy attacks. In times of war, farming families from surrounding areas could also seek refuge within the city walls. Strongholds or citadels were often built on high ground, which made them difficult to attack. In medieval Europe, many towns grew up around castles, sharing the same defenses and fortifications. Walls also allowed rulers to control who entered and left the city. At the city gates, rebels or criminals could be detained by soldiers, and visiting merchants could be taxed by officials. By the 1800s, many cities were outgrowing their surrounding walls. After the 1900s, city walls lost importance as attacks from the air became possible.

WALLS WITHIN WALLS
Carcassonne, a hilltop settlement in southwest France, was first fortified by the Celts and then the Romans. An impressive walled city during the Middle Ages, it saw heavy fighting during religious wars in the 1200s. A larger "lower town" was later built below the walls. Carcassonne's double ring of ramparts was rebuilt in the 1800s. Today, tourists admire the beautiful fortified cities and fairy-tale castles of Europe's Middle Ages, but often forget that they were the result of troubled and violent times for city-dwellers.

A traction, or human-powered, trebuchet

Sling to hold boulder

Beam swings forward when ropes are pulled

GATEWAY TO THE CITY
Walls, towers, and gates were often designed to show off a city's wealth and power. In ancient Mesopotamia (modern-day Iraq), some gateways played a significant part in religious beliefs and ceremonies. This is a reconstruction of the splendid Ishtar Gate, which was an entrance to the city of Babylon in around 575 BCE. Its blue-glazed bricks were decorated with pictures of bulls and dragons. Religious processions would pass through this gate dedicated to the goddess Ishtar on their way to the temple of the god Marduk.

Heavy timber frame for balance

Towers of San Gimignano

MEDIEVAL SKYSCRAPERS
Castles have towers because they are easy to defend and serve as lookout posts. Churches have towers to point up to heaven. During the Middle Ages, many wealthy Italian city-dwellers also made their homes in high towers, mainly to impress their neighbors. In the walled town of San Gimignano, there were about 72 tower houses, of which 14 are still standing today, looking rather like modern skyscrapers.

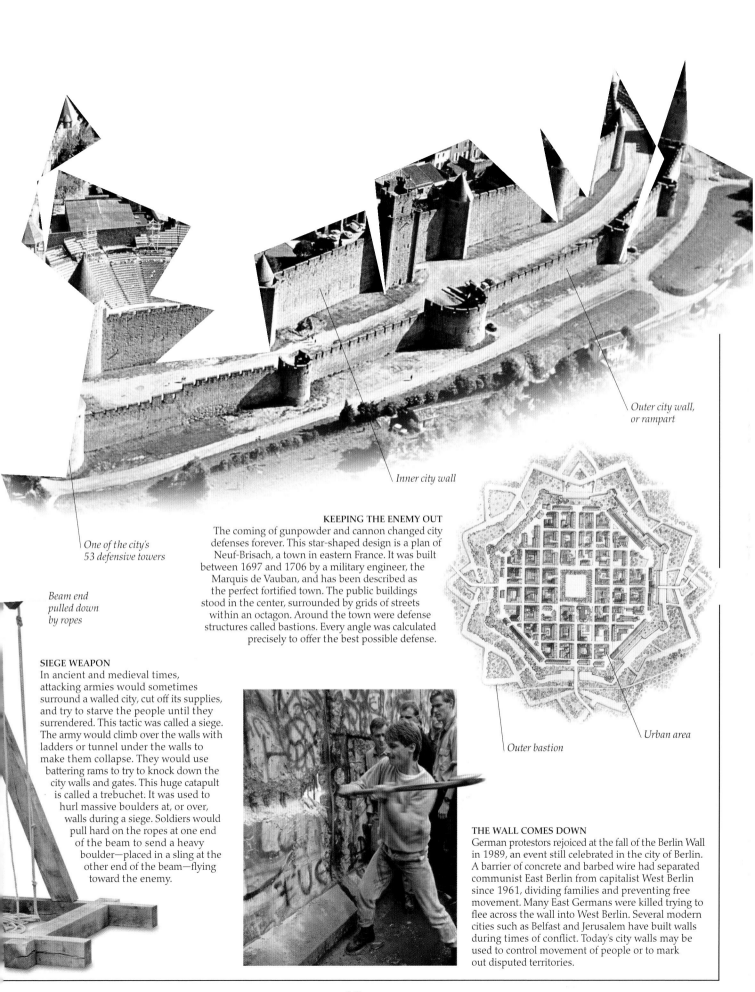

Outer city wall,
or rampart

Inner city wall

One of the city's
53 defensive towers

Beam end
pulled down
by ropes

KEEPING THE ENEMY OUT

The coming of gunpowder and cannon changed city defenses forever. This star-shaped design is a plan of Neuf-Brisach, a town in eastern France. It was built between 1697 and 1706 by a military engineer, the Marquis de Vauban, and has been described as the perfect fortified town. The public buildings stood in the center, surrounded by grids of streets within an octagon. Around the town were defense structures called bastions. Every angle was calculated precisely to offer the best possible defense.

Urban area

Outer bastion

SIEGE WEAPON

In ancient and medieval times, attacking armies would sometimes surround a walled city, cut off its supplies, and try to starve the people until they surrendered. This tactic was called a siege. The army would climb over the walls with ladders or tunnel under the walls to make them collapse. They would use battering rams to try to knock down the city walls and gates. This huge catapult is called a trebuchet. It was used to hurl massive boulders at, or over, walls during a siege. Soldiers would pull hard on the ropes at one end of the beam to send a heavy boulder—placed in a sling at the other end of the beam—flying toward the enemy.

THE WALL COMES DOWN

German protestors rejoiced at the fall of the Berlin Wall in 1989, an event still celebrated in the city of Berlin. A barrier of concrete and barbed wire had separated communist East Berlin from capitalist West Berlin since 1961, dividing families and preventing free movement. Many East Germans were killed trying to flee across the wall into West Berlin. Several modern cities such as Belfast and Jerusalem have built walls during times of conflict. Today's city walls may be used to control movement of people or to mark out disputed territories.

Trade and industry

FOR CENTURIES, CITIES HAVE BEEN THE CENTER of industry, where people make goods. However, until the 19th century, 97 percent of the world's people lived in the countryside and worked the land. From 1770 to 1850, steam-powered factories began transforming this situation in a process called the Industrial Revolution. City industry, once a matter of skilled craftspeople, handmaking pottery, cloth, and other goods, became mass production carried out by factory laborers. These workers swelled the size of cities, which often turned into forests of factory chimneys. But the revolution did not end in 1850—wave after wave of new industries triggered fresh surges of city growth in different parts of the world.

Front and back of a gold florin

THE RISE OF MONEY
During the 1100s, Europe's wealth was controlled by powerful nobles, who held all the land—even the cities. A country's economy worked for their benefit. By the 1400s, a new city-based economy had grown, founded on money and banks. It made private bankers rich and powerful. Even kings had to borrow from the banks. It was the first sign that cities could challenge the old royal power. One of the great financial centers was Florence, Italy. The city gave its name to a coin called the florin. From 1252 to 1523, florins were in use in Europe.

MEDIEVAL MANUFACTURERS
Until the Industrial Revolution, factories in cities were usually no bigger than workshops, and there was no source of power other than wind, running water, and draft animals. In medieval Europe, however, manufacturers had already formed trade associations called guilds. These protected the rights of skilled craftspeople such as stone masons, cloth makers, bakers, or carpenters. Guilds fixed prices and standards of work. As they grew rich and powerful, their influence ensured high wages for their members.

Emblem of a Dutch craft guild

SMOKING CHIMNEYS
In the late 1700s, British engineers invented efficient new steam engines that could power factories, pump water out of mines, and pull trains. Formerly, textile mills were powered by water from rivers. Now, mill owners could build them together, where there was a concentration of workers, creating the first industrial towns, such as Manchester, England, and Glasgow, Scotland. This process spread from Britain to Belgium, Germany, the US, and later the rest of the world. The new factories turned out large numbers of goods at high speed.

Mid-19th-century illustration of a factory in Sheffield, England

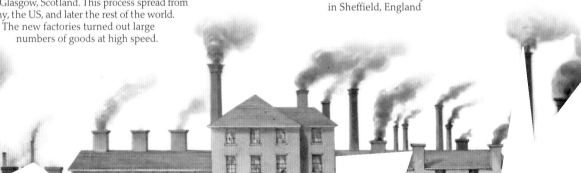

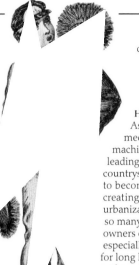

Young
chimney
sweep

HARD TIMES

As production became
mechanized in city factories,
machines transformed farming,
leading to unemployment in the
countryside. People flocked to cities
to become industrial workers,
creating the world's first major
urbanization (see pages 6–7). With
so many willing laborers, factory
owners could pay very low wages,
especially to children, who toiled
for long hours doing hazardous jobs,
such as cleaning chimneys. Pollution,
overcrowding, and poor sanitation
spread diseases such as cholera.
Public campaigns finally led to
healthier living conditions.

*Robotic arm extends
to deliver car to
waiting customer*

COMPUTER BOOM

In the 1970s, the electronics
industry sparked off new urban
growth and prosperity. Computer
firms began to set up in California
around the city of San José in
the Santa Clara Valley. This
region became known as Silicon
Valley, since silicon was used to
make microprocessors for computers.
There were new workplaces and new
homes. However, the workers were all car
owners, so rather than a dense, industrial
town, a series of spacious settlements grew up.

AUTO CITIES

New industries and new working methods developed
in the 1900s. In 1913, the US Ford Motor Company
introduced the assembly line, in which cars were
passed through lines of workers at the rate of one
every three minutes. Soon, the car industry was
triggering a period of boom for US cities, including
Detroit, Michigan, the "Motor City" or "Motown," and
whole cities were built just to make cars, such as
Dearborn, Michigan, and Wolfsburg, Germany.
Today, Wolfsburg celebrates its car-making heritage
with a visitors' center featuring "car towers."
Customers can pick up their new Volkswagen
cars from these robotically stacked towers,
which hold 400 cars on 20 levels.

Computer
circuit boards

Rubber gloves in a
Malaysian factory

THE REVOLUTION CONTINUES
Many countries, including Malaysia,
remained relatively poor and rural,
because industrialized countries
bought only their raw agricultural
goods, such as rubber. From the 1970s,
Malaysia became industrial, building
factories to manufacture products such
as rubber gloves from its raw materials.
It began exporting these with added
value, creating more wealth. As in
Europe in the 1800s, industrialization led
to urbanization. The Klang region around
Malaysia's capital Kuala Lumpur has
grown into a conurbation of 6 million
inhabitants. The company that owns this
factory near Klang is the world's largest
manufacturer of rubber gloves. Malaysia
now exports motor vehicles, electronics,
and textiles, and is today a leading
economy in Southeast Asia.

Cities at war

CITIES ARE KEY military targets in wars and conflicts. Seizing control of a city can bring political power and wealth. Destroying the city of an enemy can lead to their defeat. In 146 BCE, the Romans sacked the city of Carthage in North Africa, razing it to the ground. The Carthaginians never regained their power. When two armies fight on the battlefield, soldiers are killed. However, when a city is attacked, everyone, even children and the elderly, is at risk of injury or death. During a medieval siege, citizens often starved to death. Those who resisted the enemy were often slaughtered if the city was captured. During the 20th century, aircraft and heavy artillery could rain down bombs and shells on cities, destroying property and killing thousands.

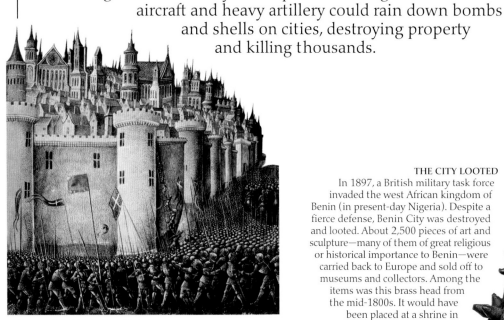

THE SIEGE AS A WEAPON
This painting from the 1400s shows the siege of Antioch, Syria. This took place from 1097 to 1098, when Christian armies tried to capture the city held by Muslim Turks. There was starvation and terrible bloodshed within the city. Probably the worst siege in history took place between 1941 and 1943, during World War II (1939–45). The German army sealed off the Russian city of Leningrad, now St. Petersburg, and about 1.5 million citizens died of famine.

THE CITY LOOTED
In 1897, a British military task force invaded the west African kingdom of Benin (in present-day Nigeria). Despite a fierce defense, Benin City was destroyed and looted. About 2,500 pieces of art and sculpture—many of them of great religious or historical importance to Benin—were carried back to Europe and sold off to museums and collectors. Among the items was this brass head from the mid-1800s. It would have been placed at a shrine in the palace of the *oba*, or king, of Benin.

Headdress of coral and agate

High necklace of coral beads

THE PEOPLE RISE UP
Warfare often breaks out within cities during uprisings or civil wars. In 1871, the commune (city council) in Paris declared its own independent, democratic government, known as the Paris Commune. It adopted revolutionary policies, attempting to give power to the working class and women. Its supporters fought against the French government's troops on the streets. When the government regained military control of Paris, tens of thousands of supporters of the Commune were executed, imprisoned, or exiled.

Medal issued by the Paris Commune

ATTACK FROM THE AIR

Just eight years after the first powered flight in 1903, the Italians were using planes in warfare. During World War II, bombs rained down on European cities such as London, Rotterdam, Berlin, Cologne, and Dresden, causing massive destruction, injury, and death. These Flying Fortress bombers of the United States Air Force dropped bombs on an industrial city in Germany in December 1944.

REMEMBERING HIROSHIMA

In August 1945, US aircraft dropped atomic bombs on the cities of Hiroshima and Nagasaki in Japan, destroying them immediately. Tens of thousands of civilians died instantly in a blinding flash of light and fire. Many others died horribly from sickness caused by atomic radiation in the months and years that followed. In modern Hiroshima, the Genbaku Dome, one of the few buildings that survived, has been preserved as a Peace Memorial.

SOLDIERS ON THE STREETS

US Marines patrol the streets of Mogadishu, Somalia, in 1993 during a conflict between US troops and Somali militia fighters. Modern warfare in cities is often fought between groups of fighters and professional soldiers, using guns, tanks, armored personnel carriers, rocket-propelled grenades, bombs, and tear gas. During city warfare, essential goods may not be available, and emergency services may not be able to reach the victims. Ambushes, street-by-street fighting, or raids run a high risk of injuring or killing innocent civilians.

The South Tower, seconds after being struck by a hijacked aircraft

TERROR IN NEW YORK CITY

On September 11, 2001, terrorists flew hijacked aircraft into the twin towers of the World Trade Center in New York City. This horrific attack killed about 2,600 people, and it was just one of several carried out in the US on that day. Terrorism is an attempt by individuals, groups, or states to bring about political change by instilling fear in people's minds. In a city, high-rise buildings, public transportation, and crowded places make terrorist attacks especially dangerous.

City zones

HISTORIC HEART
Chandni Chowk is a bustling trading area within the walled city of Old Delhi, at the heart of the Indian capital. Founded in 1648, it has grown over the centuries to accommodate markets dealing in everything from jewelry and spices to utensils and dry fruits. Besides the countless stores along its narrow lanes, there are also houses, mosques, and temples in the area.

THE VARIOUS DISTRICTS OF A CITY fit together like pieces of a giant jigsaw puzzle. The city center, or downtown area, may be divided between centers of government and business and various shopping or entertainment districts. Many cities have an old town or historical core, such as the Gothic Quarter in Barcelona, Spain, or Vieux-Montréal, the oldest area in the city of Montréal, Canada. Housing areas can be set apart from each other by their wealth or poverty, or by the style of their architecture. They can be fashionable or run-down. Suburbs may have been specially built to house city workers, or might be smaller towns swallowed up by the growth of the city. Factories were once built in the middle of cities, but today are generally grouped in industrial zones on the outskirts.

AMP Tower

UPHILL AND DOWNHILL

The shape of the land can create separate city districts. San Francisco in California is grouped around more than 50 steep hills. The city's historic cable cars climb some of them, like this car on Russian Hill in the northeast district by the San Francisco Bay. A particular part of a city can be separated from the others by hills, valleys, lakes, islands, or rivers. As a result, one district may have to rely on ferries, bridges, or tunnels to link up with the others. These different city areas may even experience different local weather conditions.

THE BUSINESS HUB

City centers are commercial centers that often have the tallest and most spectacular buildings in town, a consequence of high land prices and the high density of office workers. The AMP Tower in Sydney, Australia, is 1,000 ft (305 m) high and attracts a million visitors each year. It overlooks Sydney's central business district (CBD) and the shoreline where the city was founded by British colonists in 1788. The CBD is a center of international banking, finance, and insurance. Across the harbor from the CBD are mainly residential neighbourhoods, where people who work in the CBD may have their houses.

WELCOME TO CHINATOWN

City districts may take their character from the ethnic background of the people who live there. Since the 1800s, Chinese people have settled in cities around the world. Originally working as laborers, seamen, or traders, their descendants still often live in the same districts, known as Chinatowns. These areas have Chinese restaurants, grocery stores, bookshops, and craft stores. Chinese festivals, celebrated with lion dances, firecrackers, and clashing cymbals, attract many tourists.

Chinese paper lantern

Budapest crest shows the two castles of Buda and Pest

JOINED-UP CITIES

The districts that make up a modern city today might have once been separate towns or even cities that merged, or were united politically. The Hungarian capital Budapest was originally two separate settlements—Buda, on the west bank of the Danube River, and Pest on the east bank. The two were formally united in 1873. In Germany, Berlin merged with its neighbor Cölln, while in England, the city of London crept westward along the banks of the Thames River to take in Westminster.

THE POVERTY GAP

The sharpest and most noticeable difference between city districts is often that between wealth and poverty. The Makati City district of greater Manila in the Philippines is the center of that nation's financial and banking system. Yet within a short distance of its gleaming skyscrapers, poor families struggle to survive from one day to the next in crowded and dirty shacks. Poor districts like this often rise up wherever land is vacant or unwanted in a city.

Urban anatomy

AZTEC PLANNERS
Tenochtitlan was founded by the Aztecs in 1325, on an island in a lake. This is now the site of Mexico City. The city's planners divided the Aztec capital into four zones and joined it to the mainland by causeways (raised roads). They built islands in the lake's shallow waters to grow crops. When the Spanish invaded in 1519, they were astounded by the city's temples and palaces.

MANY ANCIENT CITIES developed over the centuries as a complex maze of streets. This layout is sometimes preserved to this day. Old north African towns, for instance, often have a central jumble of alleyways called a medina. However, the layouts of cities can also be planned. More than 4,000 years ago, the streets of Indus Valley cities (in present-day Pakistan) were laid out in a rectangular grid pattern. Cities have contrasting layouts, but they can also appear different due to architecture (building design), and this varies with cultural traditions, the climate, and the local building materials available.

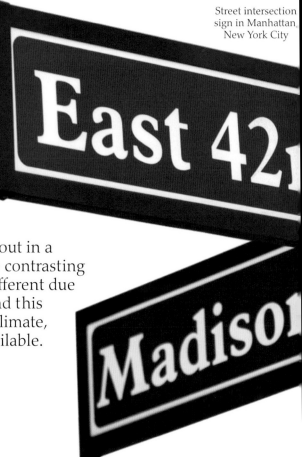

Street intersection sign in Manhattan, New York City

RADIAL PARIS
Twelve broad avenues radiate from the Arc de Triomphe, a great monument at the center of the French capital. In the 1850s, large areas of medieval Paris were pulled down to make way for a more spacious city, with new water mains and sewers, new bridges, and grand buildings. The changes were devised by the town planner Georges-Eugène Haussmann (1809–91). The wide streets were designed to improve communications and move troops across the city more quickly. The result is the Paris that people know today.

VERTICAL PLANNING

Cities grow upward as well as sideways, and planning the height of buildings is as important as planning the area they occupy. These high-rise homes in Shibam, a desert city in Yemen, were raised between 1553 and the 1800s. They were built high and close together so that they could be easily defended from hostile desert tribes. The houses are 5 to 11 stories high and are built from dried mud bricks on stone foundations.

GRIDS AND BLOCKS

The grid plan became popular in US cities in the 1800s. The roads in New York City intersect (meet and cross) at right angles forming a grid, with the spaces in between filled by built-up blocks of offices, stores, and housing. Grids make the maximum use of land, and street names such as East 42nd Street help visitors know exactly where they are. The city blocks in Manhattan in New York City have a standard size of 265 by 900 ft (80 by 275 m). However, the large number of intersections slows down traffic, with lines of cars filling the streets with exhaust fumes.

CANALS OF VENICE

The Italian city of Venice grew up between the 700s and 1300s. It was built on islands in a shallow coastal lagoon. There was no room for large roads, so the city became crisscrossed with a maze of alleys, bridges, and canals. Buildings were supported by wooden piles, driven into the mud. The intricate medieval city layout remains today, and canals still offer the easiest way of delivering goods to businesses and homes.

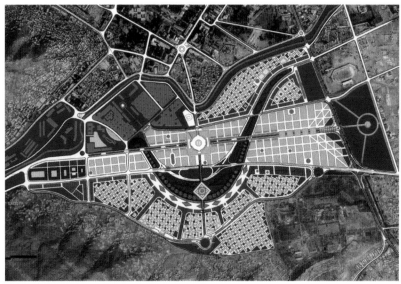

PLANNING FOR RENEWAL

Many cities are rebuilt according to new plans after they have been destroyed in war. This development plan for Kabul, the ancient city and present capital of Afghanistan, was prepared in 2004. The city had been devastated by decades of warfare. Ongoing conflict still hinders new development. This plan aimed to protect historic buildings while creating new bridges and roads, a new water supply and transportation system, as well as parks and markets.

- ■ Historic structures
- ■ Medical facilities
- ▨ Commercial/retail area
- ▨ Housing units
- ■ Apartment blocks
- ■ Green area

High-rise

PEOPLE HAVE BEEN BUILDING high for
more than 7,000 years. Massive pyramids and
temple mounds were raised in Asia and Africa in ancient
times. In the Americas, too, the Mayan and Aztec people built
their cities around sacred pyramids. Modern high-rise buildings still
use their size and height to impress the onlooker and they are still built
in prime locations, which are now the central business districts of cities
(see pages 24–25). The opportunity to build really tall structures came
in the 1850s with improvements in the manufacture of iron, steel, and
glass, and the invention of the elevator. A great fire destroyed Chicago
in 1871, and this gave architects a chance to experiment
with new steel-framed high-rises. Today's tallest
building is the Burj Khalifa in Dubai that
soars to 2,715 ft (828 m).

Smaller upper tier

Reconstructed facade with staircase

Massive bottom tier

WHY BUILD HIGH?
Tall buildings, like these on New York City's 6th Avenue, are built
to make a statement. They can demonstrate the wealth of a big
corporation or show off the importance of a city's business
district. The most centrally located and prestigious areas
in any city are also the most expensive, as in Manhattan in
New York City, because they are in such demand.
Building upward in these places is a cheaper and
more efficient use of space than building
outward. However, skyscrapers do not
always create a friendly city atmosphere.
Deep canyons of concrete can block out
sunshine, and the grand scale can
sometimes be intimidating from below.

The Ziggurat
of Ur

THE FIRST HIGH-RISES
In ancient Iraq, temple platforms called
ziggurats towered over cities such as Ur.
These brick mountains, some built more than
4,000 years ago, were meant to be homes for the
gods. A ziggurat in Babylon that rose 300 ft (91 m)
in seven great tiers (stories) may have been the
basis of ancient tales about a "Tower of Babel."
The version in the Bible tells how the people of the
world tried to build a tower to reach the heavens, but
God punished them for their overreaching ambition
by making them speak in different languages, so that
they could no longer understand each other.

THE PIONEERS
The 1930s was a period of intense skyscraper construction in New York City. The Empire State Building touched 1,250 ft (381 m) in 1931, taking over as the world's tallest building from the Chrysler Building at 1,047 ft (319 m). In 1932, these construction workers helped to build the RCA Building in the Rockefeller Center complex. Now known as the GE Building, it is 70 stories tall. In the early days of skyscraper construction, workers did not wear safety harnesses or hard hats, as they must today, and would be at home taking a lunch break on a steel girder 800 ft (245 m) above the ground.

HIGH-RISE HOUSING
Most skyscrapers initially served as offices. From the 1950s onward, architects adapted high-rise designs to housing projects, such as this one in Germany. However, new high-rise apartments were sometimes poorly and cheaply designed. Their prefabricated concrete slabs quickly became shabby. Children didn't have enough space to play or exercise, stores were far away, and elderly people became isolated from their neighbors, since they could not easily move up and down the buildings.

Structure: 1,485 ft (452 m)

Foundation: 395 ft (120 m)

Petronas Towers, Kuala Lumpur, Malaysia

50 ft (15 m) of basement and parking

15 ft (4.5 m) raft of reinforced concrete

WINDY CITY
Architects must make sure that skyscrapers fit in with other buildings in the area. They should not block out sunlight, or create turbulent air currents. People disagree as to why Chicago became known as the Windy City, but already in the 1890s people had noticed that the city's skyscrapers acted as cliffs, funneling winds down into the streets. High-rise buildings tend to channel strong gusts and eddies of wind in between them, whipping up dust or litter.

ROOTED IN ROCK
The techniques used to anchor skyscrapers to the ground depend on the geology of a city. Hard bedrock makes an ideal foundation. Workers drive pillars of steel or concrete, known as piles or piers, into the rock. On softer surfaces, such as clay or shale, they may use great rafts of steel-reinforced concrete. The twin Petronas Towers rising above the city of Kuala Lumpur, Malaysia, have the world's deepest foundations, comprising thick rafts of concrete and deep piles that go down into the soft bedrock.

Longest piles are 345 ft (105m) deep

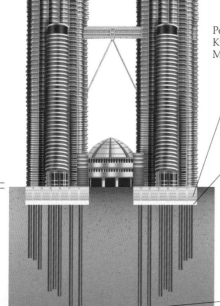

Urban sprawl

ANCIENT AND MEDIEVAL CITIES were confined within their walls (see pages 18–19), but modern cities sprawl outward, swallowing up smaller settlements as they grow. Beyond the skyscrapers and historic districts of the central city, there are large areas of housing for commuters and towns that are "satellites" of the city itself. In Europe, the word suburb refers to any outer residential district of a city. In North America, suburbs are outlying urban areas that are not governed by the central city authority. In developing countries, outer districts may include shanty towns—unplanned, unofficial housing built by poor migrants to the city. In densely populated countries, cities may end up merging into each other, creating vast urban regions called conurbations.

ESCAPE FROM THE CITY
In the 19th and 20th centuries, people started moving from the inner city to the outer districts, which were greener and less crowded, yet within traveling distance of their jobs in the inner city. This was made possible by the development of railroads and motor transportation. Here, a London Underground poster from 1908 advertises a new suburban development. The railroads, to increase their revenues, encouraged people to move to the suburbs.

INTERCONNECTIONS
Urban sprawl is generated by transportation. Most big modern cities are designed for the car, with networks of multilane urban freeways and slip roads. These are designed to provide speedy links between central districts and outlying areas. However, freeways may isolate parts of the city, creating areas of "urban blight," where people do not want to live. Building bigger, faster roads tends to encourage people to make more car trips. It also encourages developers to build housing and shopping malls on cheap land on the remote outskirts of town. The demand for more roads just increases and the city expands.

SEA OF ROOFS
Beyond the high-rise towers of downtown Los Angeles, California, the city extends over a vast sprawl of low-rise residential districts and suburbs, covering some 500 sq miles (1,300 sq km). Los Angeles is the second-most populous city in the US, with 3.8 million inhabitants—but its surrounding urban area is home to about 15 million. The task facing city planners is how to make large and diverse areas of a city work together as a whole. City planners design street layouts, housing, shopping and industrial areas, parks, and transportation systems. They try to create thriving communities within the city.

CONURBATION
Seen from space, a conurbation or mega-city looks like an immense, ever-expanding concrete sprawl. This is Greater Tokyo—the region around Japan's capital city. Tokyo has overflowed into the neighboring regions of Chiba, Saitama, and Kanagawa, creating the world's largest urban area, covering some 5,300 sq miles (13,750 sq km)—nearly as large as the state of Connecticut. This mega-city is home to 35 million people—or 28 percent of Japan's population.

SPILLOVER
In many overcrowded cities next to rivers or the sea, it is common for urban sprawl to extend over water, creating suburbs of houseboats and floating marketplaces. Beneath the skyscrapers of Hong Kong harbor's Aberdeen district, traditional Chinese boats such as junks and sampans house about 6,000 people. Fifty years ago, this community numbered about 150,000. The boat-dwellers depend on fishing, and overfishing in the Pearl River delta region has led to their declining numbers.

ON THE EDGE
In 2005, riots broke out in a poor district in the eastern suburbs of Paris and soon spread to suburbs in other French cities. The social unrest followed rising tensions between young people and the police. Cars and buildings were burned. While some outlying urban areas may be prosperous and peaceful, this is not always the case. Rising rents or property prices can drive poor families out of the inner city. In the suburbs, they are likely to find themselves marginalized and pushed to the edges of society.

People pressure

IN 1900, ONLY 16 CITIES HAD A POPULATION greater than 1 million, but today there are more than 400. Many people move to cities from rural areas to find work. This process is known as urbanization, and it is happening more quickly today than ever before. Urban growth can benefit the economies of developing countries, such as China and India, because the influx of people provides a source of workers for new industries. Most newcomers arrive in search of better wages and housing, but may find neither. Today, some cities' populations are growing so fast that huge strains are placed on their infrastructure—the facilities and services needed to support the community, such as roads, sewers, and water supply.

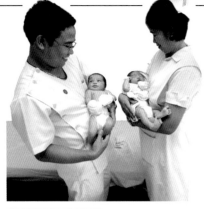

GROWING NUMBERS
These newborn babies at a hospital in Manila in the Philippines have just joined the city's growing population of 12 million people. City-dwellers use up a lot of resources such as water, and the industries employing them use even more. This has already led to water rationing in Manila.

SHORT OF SPACE
In a booming city with a growing population, demand for land and living space becomes intense. In the key locations near central railroad stations, prices rocket. In Japanese cities such as Osaka (above) and Tokyo, the affordable answer is capsule hotels. Instead of renting a pricey apartment or hotel room, business people working away from home often check in to a pod barely bigger than a coffin. A hotel may contain hundreds of these compartments, along with lockers and shared bathroom facilities.

LOOKING FOR A BETTER LIFE
These migrants from Africa put to sea in search of a better life in the wealthy cities of Europe. Just as the search for work drives people from the country to towns, so poverty drives many people from developing countries across international borders. Many are also trying to escape other forces beyond their control, such as famine, war, or terrorism. The migrants who get through often seek illegal work in big cities, where they risk deportation by the authorities or exploitation by criminals.

ONE IS ENOUGH
A poster in Guangzhou, China, urges couples to have just one child. This has been Chinese government policy since 1978. The prohibition is aimed at city-dwellers, who can be fined if they have a second baby. The goal is to reduce population growth. It has prevented millions of births, but in turn has created social problems, like a growing number of spoiled single children, commonly known as the "little emperors."

SHANTY TOWNS
Many cities in the developing world are flooded with desperately poor migrants from the countryside. Most set up home in districts of homemade shacks and shelters, often erected illegally. These areas are known by various names, such as shanty town, slum, or favela, in different countries. Kibera is a shanty town outside the Kenyan capital Nairobi, bordering the railroad line to Uganda. Between 250,000 and 800,000 people live here, in an area of just 1 sq mile (2.5 sq km). Living conditions are wretched and unhealthy, and the site is often flooded. A nine-year program to relocate the people of Kibera and other Nairobi slums began in 2009.

SHRINKING CITIES
Economics can make a city grow and thrive, but can also do the reverse—a process called urban decay. In the 1950s, Detroit was the prosperous center of the US car-manufacturing industry. A long decline began when people started moving out into the suburbs, which seemed more peaceful and crime-free. The inner-city housing market collapsed. By 2000, after decades of deterioration in the US car industry, the central city population was at half its 1950 level, and hundreds of buildings stood empty. This was once a grand hotel, then a block of luxury apartments. It closed in the 1990s and was abandoned and vandalized. Planners are now undertaking the regeneration of the city.

COUNTING PEOPLE
A census is a population count usually organized every 10 years. The data collected during a census tells planners how quickly a city is growing, or shrinking. It can also provide other useful "demographic" data about age, gender, occupation, and family size. Many cities are now growing at breakneck speed. This demographic chart shows that Bangalore is one of the fastest-growing cities in India. This is because of the city's rapid economic growth, largely based on the computer industry.

Population (in millions)

Year	Population
1971	1.66
1981	2.92
1991	4.13
2001	5.68
2011*	7.34

Year

*Estimated data

Come together

CITIES ARE SOCIABLE PLACES where people can make friends, work, study, shop, or have fun. That is one reason why cities exist, and why they attract newcomers. A successful city is one that brings people together. However, city communities may also be fragmented, separated by wealth, age, ethnic background, or religion. Social divisions can make individuals feel powerless, excluded, or lonely. City society can break down due to street crime, vandalism, or homelessness. These are often related to wider issues such as a lack of employment or affordable housing. City planners try to help cities function well. They can make sure that major roads do not cut off one community from another. They can create public areas that encourage social interaction but discourage crime.

ALONE IN A CROWD
In small towns or villages, most people are known to their community. Neighbors can keep an eye on the elderly or the vulnerable. They can contact relatives in an emergency. In big cities with millions of citizens, it is much easier to ignore individuals. People do not know the personal background of strangers, who are no more than faces in the crowd.

MISSING PERSONS
These identification details belong to young people who have gone missing. They have been printed on milk cartons in the hope that a member of the public will recognize a face or a name. Around 2 million teenagers run away from home in the US every year, and many head to nearby cities. Some end up sleeping on the streets, where they are especially vulnerable to crime, depression, or violence.

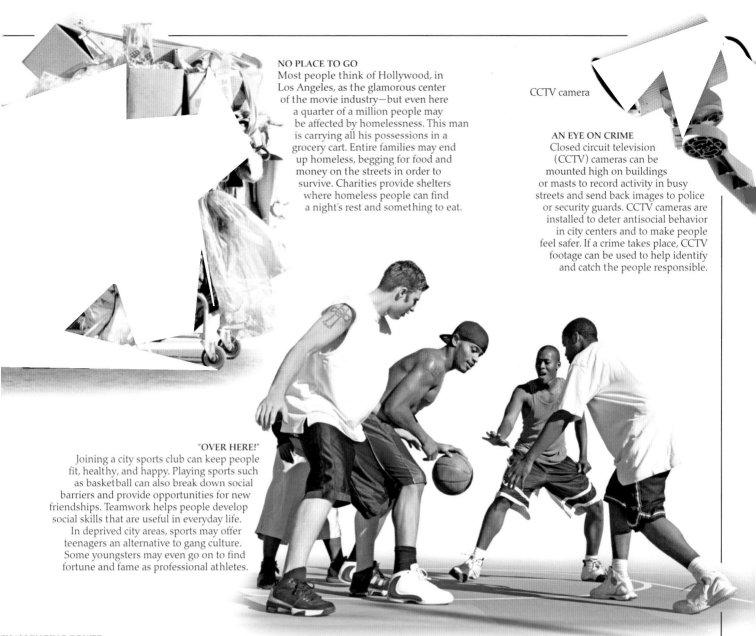

NO PLACE TO GO
Most people think of Hollywood, in Los Angeles, as the glamorous center of the movie industry—but even here a quarter of a million people may be affected by homelessness. This man is carrying all his possessions in a grocery cart. Entire families may end up homeless, begging for food and money on the streets in order to survive. Charities provide shelters where homeless people can find a night's rest and something to eat.

CCTV camera

AN EYE ON CRIME
Closed circuit television (CCTV) cameras can be mounted high on buildings or masts to record activity in busy streets and send back images to police or security guards. CCTV cameras are installed to deter antisocial behavior in city centers and to make people feel safer. If a crime takes place, CCTV footage can be used to help identify and catch the people responsible.

"OVER HERE!"
Joining a city sports club can keep people fit, healthy, and happy. Playing sports such as basketball can also break down social barriers and provide opportunities for new friendships. Teamwork helps people develop social skills that are useful in everyday life. In deprived city areas, sports may offer teenagers an alternative to gang culture. Some youngsters may even go on to find fortune and fame as professional athletes.

CHALLENGING POWER
Protestors wearing red shirts and waving red flags took to the streets of Bangkok, the capital of Thailand, in 2010, to protest against the country's government. Many cities are centers of government and state power, and because of this they are often the focus of protest marches, political rallies, and demonstrations calling for social change. In a free society, people have the right to protest and make their views known. However, some governments use police or troops to attack their critics on the city streets.

Red shirt protestors in Bangkok

GETTING TO KNOW YOU
Paris is famous for its cafés. Their attraction is not just the food or coffee that they serve, but also the social atmosphere that they create. They provide somewhere to sit down in a busy city, a chance to read the newspaper or a guidebook, a place to meet up with friends and gossip. Creating an area of cafés and fashionable small shops can bring life back to parts of a city where markets or factories have closed down.

The city at work

CITY OFFICES
Every day people commute to the offices of large companies or small businesses to provide services to customers. Since the 1970s, the computer has altered the way people work and connect with each other. Although communications technology has brought people all over the world closer, virtual interaction by computer is taking the place of face-to-face communication.

ECONOMIC FORCES CREATED THE FIRST CITIES, when people first came to live and work together, trading their goods and services with one another. Some modern city-dwellers still work in manufacturing, but in wealthier countries, most people work in service industries, such as banking, insurance, or retail (selling goods in stores). Companies tend to site their factories in the outskirts of cities, but their headquarters occupy skyscrapers in the city centers. Wealth creation in cities can be measured by their Gross Domestic Product (GDP), or the value of all goods and services they produce in a year. In Japan, the total GDP of Tokyo is around $1.5 trillion—nearly five times that of the entire nation of Zimbabwe.

FASHION FOCUS
In the world's fashion capitals, spring and fall shows by leading designers point the way forward for the fashion industry. The shows promote the image of the city as a fashionable and exciting place and present it as an industry leader, attracting trade from across the globe. Paris has been at the cutting edge of fashion for more than 400 years and is today joined by cities such as Milan, London, and New York.

Model at Milan
Fashion Week,
Italy

CENTERS OF FINANCE
In a global economy, the financial news from one city immediately affects every other city on the planet. New York City's Wall Street is a major center of world finance, being home to the New York Stock Exchange (NYSE). Traders gather on the floor of the exchange to buy and sell stocks and shares. A day's trading can be worth up to $153 billion. Speculation, or placing bets, on the future price of commodities, such as metals, is another multibillion dollar business. It is based at the New York Mercantile Exchange. Financial cities including New York, London, Hong Kong, Singapore, and Zurich now work as global marketplaces for the world's trade.

CINEMA CITIES

First of all, there was Hollywood, which became a world center of film and entertainment in the early 20th century. Then there was Mumbai (formerly Bombay) in India, which became the capital of a hugely successful Hindi-language film industry, earning itself the nickname Bollywood. This 2008 movie poster comes from another cinema city—Hong Kong. From the 1970s onward, Hong Kong has become internationally famous for Chinese martial arts films, thanks to actors such as Bruce Lee and Jackie Chan.

HIGH-RISE CLEANERS

Window cleaning can be dangerous work amid the new city towers of Shanghai, China. City businesses employ large numbers of people in supporting work such as cleaning, maintenance, repairs, security, driving, or communications. Many of these jobs are low profile and are performed outside of normal working hours. Even so, the city depends on these workers so it can function from one day to the next. Low wages are a problem for many city-dwellers, but in some countries they may enjoy the protection of a legal minimum wage.

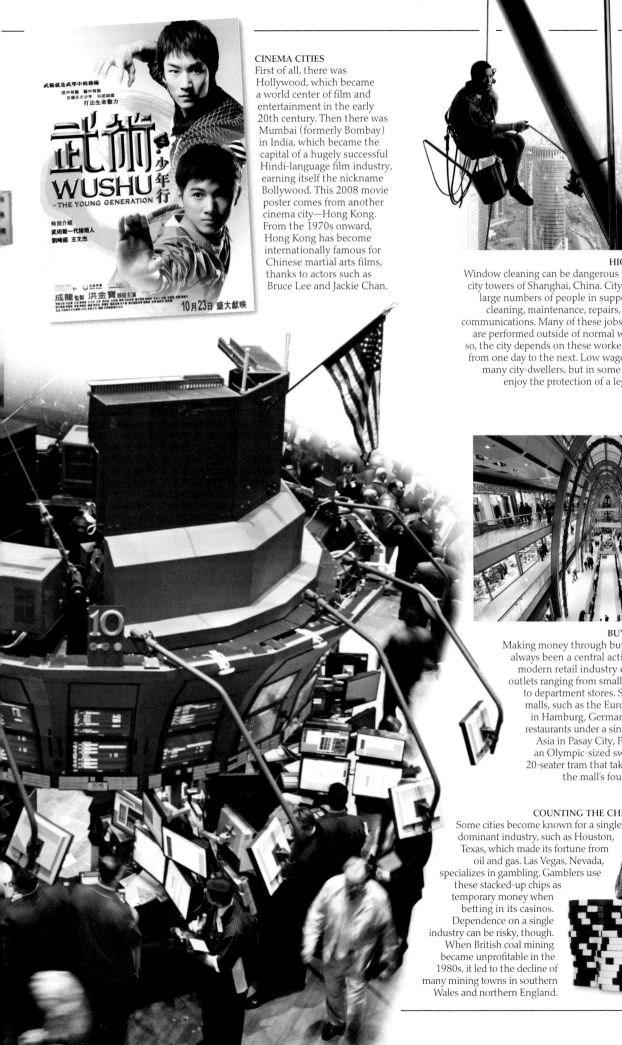

BUYING AND SELLING

Making money through buying and selling has always been a central activity of city life. The modern retail industry employs workers in outlets ranging from small independent shops to department stores. Shopping centers, or malls, such as the Europa Passage (above) in Hamburg, Germany, house stores and restaurants under a single roof. The Mall of Asia in Pasay City, Philippines, includes an Olympic-sized swimming pool and a 20-seater tram that takes shoppers around the mall's four gigantic buildings.

COUNTING THE CHIPS

Some cities become known for a single dominant industry, such as Houston, Texas, which made its fortune from oil and gas. Las Vegas, Nevada, specializes in gambling. Gamblers use these stacked-up chips as temporary money when betting in its casinos. Dependence on a single industry can be risky, though. When British coal mining became unprofitable in the 1980s, it led to the decline of many mining towns in southern Wales and northern England.

On the move

IN THE DAYS WHEN MOST PEOPLE walked to work, cities were much smaller in area. In the 1st century CE, it was possible to walk across Roman London in 20 minutes. In the 19th century, the coming of rail and motorized transportation led to a rapid expansion, creating new suburbs for commuters. Today, London's greater urban area would take 11 hours to cross by foot. Modern cities are a maze of highways, flyovers, railroads, and tunnels, all aiming to provide rapid transit. Some cities benefit from traffic-free areas for pedestrians and pedestrian-free areas for traffic. Planners try to ensure that transportation systems interconnect, so that people, vehicles, and goods can move quickly into, out of, or across, town.

WHO GOES WHERE?
The London Underground, popularly known as "the Tube," was the world's first underground railroad and has connected the city since 1863. It now links suburbs with the center, railroad stations with airports, and hotels with tourist districts, providing swift transit beneath the city's traffic-filled, congested streets. The system has about 250 miles (400 km) of track, and its 270 stations handle 1 billion passengers each year.

KEEP IT FLOWING!
Passengers use these electronic passes on all types of public transportation in Istanbul, Turkey. The passes prevent the delays of buying and validating lots of separate tickets. Traffic flow through clogged streets can be eased in other ways. City authorities may boost public transportation by dedicating one lane of the street to buses and setting up park-and-ride programs, in which drivers park on the city limits and ride the bus into the center. In Durham, England, traffic has reduced by 90 percent since private drivers were first charged to enter the city's historic core.

Akbil transit passes

THE JAM
The traffic jam is not just a product of the motorized age. Wagons and carts blocked the markets of ancient Rome, and the horse carriages of Victorian London often came to a standstill long before the days of the car. This scene shows a busy street intersection in Paris in about 1912, with cars, carriages, and pedestrians jostling for space.

ABOVE THE STREETS
Monorail trains run on a single rail. They often carry passengers high above city streets, freeing up space at ground level. The Metro Monorail in Sydney, Australia, is powered by electric motors and glides along on rubber wheels. The 2.2-mile (3.6-km) track links Darling Harbour with Chinatown, the main shopping area, and the central business district (see pages 24–25). It is popular with tourists visiting the city. Monorails have become landmarks in cities around the world, from Düsseldorf, Germany to Tokyo, Japan.

PEDAL POWER

This *becak* (pronounced bay-cha) on the streets of Yogyakarta city is an Indonesian version of the cycle rickshaw. It is a combination of a rickshaw (a traditional Asian handcart for passengers) and a bicycle. This is a cheap and pollution-free mode of public transportation. Many Asian countries also have autorickshaws, or motorized versions of cycle rickshaws.

LL ABOARD

Most riverside cities make use of water transportation. Ferry boats allow city commuters to make short cuts to work across rivers or harbors. This passenger ferry links Staten Island with Manhattan, New York City. The 5-mile (8-km) crossing takes 25 minutes, and the city lays on the service free of charge. Public transportation services often shut down at night, but the Staten Island ferry runs 24 hours a day.

UNDER THE SMOG

Smog (a mixture of smoke and fog) is a type of air pollution created by exhaust fumes from traffic and smoke from factories. Los Angeles, California, is a city designed for cars. Major freeways crisscross the city and only 11 percent of commuters travel to work on public transportation. A blanket of smog often lies over the city. Local laws require residents to drive low-polluting cars to help reduce smog levels.

HARBOUR-LINK TNT

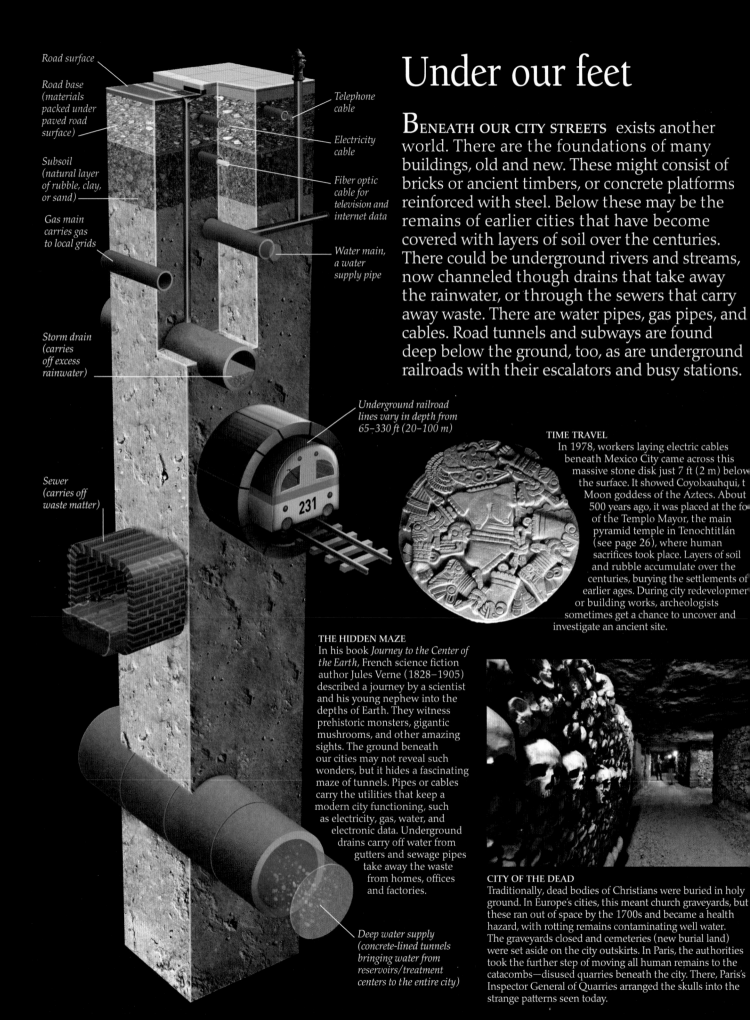

Under our feet

BENEATH OUR CITY STREETS exists another world. There are the foundations of many buildings, old and new. These might consist of bricks or ancient timbers, or concrete platforms reinforced with steel. Below these may be the remains of earlier cities that have become covered with layers of soil over the centuries. There could be underground rivers and streams, now channeled though drains that take away the rainwater, or through the sewers that carry away waste. There are water pipes, gas pipes, and cables. Road tunnels and subways are found deep below the ground, too, as are underground railroads with their escalators and busy stations.

Road surface

Road base (materials packed under paved road surface)

Subsoil (natural layer of rubble, clay, or sand)

Gas main carries gas to local grids

Storm drain (carries off excess rainwater)

Sewer (carries off waste matter)

Telephone cable

Electricity cable

Fiber optic cable for television and internet data

Water main, a water supply pipe

Underground railroad lines vary in depth from 65–330 ft (20–100 m)

231

Deep water supply (concrete-lined tunnels bringing water from reservoirs/treatment centers to the entire city)

TIME TRAVEL
In 1978, workers laying electric cables beneath Mexico City came across this massive stone disk just 7 ft (2 m) below the surface. It showed Coyolxauhqui, t Moon goddess of the Aztecs. About 500 years ago, it was placed at the fo of the Templo Mayor, the main pyramid temple in Tenochtitlán (see page 26), where human sacrifices took place. Layers of soil and rubble accumulate over the centuries, burying the settlements of earlier ages. During city redevelopmer or building works, archeologists sometimes get a chance to uncover and investigate an ancient site.

THE HIDDEN MAZE
In his book *Journey to the Center of the Earth*, French science fiction author Jules Verne (1828–1905) described a journey by a scientist and his young nephew into the depths of Earth. They witness prehistoric monsters, gigantic mushrooms, and other amazing sights. The ground beneath our cities may not reveal such wonders, but it hides a fascinating maze of tunnels. Pipes or cables carry the utilities that keep a modern city functioning, such as electricity, gas, water, and electronic data. Underground drains carry off water from gutters and sewage pipes take away the waste from homes, offices and factories.

CITY OF THE DEAD
Traditionally, dead bodies of Christians were buried in holy ground. In Europe's cities, this meant church graveyards, but these ran out of space by the 1700s and became a health hazard, with rotting remains contaminating well water. The graveyards closed and cemeteries (new burial land) were set aside on the city outskirts. In Paris, the authorities took the further step of moving all human remains to the catacombs—disused quarries beneath the city. There, Paris's Inspector General of Quarries arranged the skulls into the strange patterns seen today.

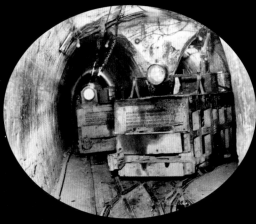

MAIL RAIL

In around 1900, the Chicago Tunnel Company built several small tunnels beneath the city of Chicago to create a network for carrying telephone cables. It built a unique miniature railroad to remove excavated rock and then to pull the cables through. When work was over, the little railroad engines found new life carrying wagons of letters and packages around the city at high speed. Britain's Royal Mail adopted a similar system with its own Mail Rail, which ran from 1927 to 2003.

LET IT FLOW

Beneath the city of Kakusabe in the Saitama region of Greater Tokyo (see page 31) is a drainage system capable of dealing with the severe flooding created by typhoons and storms during Japan's rainy season. The G-Cans project includes 40 miles (64 km) of tunnels, built about 165 ft (50 m) below greater Tokyo. Water can be contained in five huge concrete silos, and fed into a gigantic pillared tank, seen above. This water can then be pumped out into the Edo River at the incredible rate of some 200 tons (180 metric tons) per second.

Cutting edge

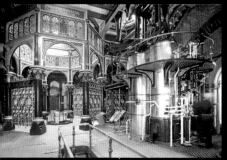

THE GREAT STINK

In 1858, people in London had to hold their noses due to the foul stench rising from the Thames River, which was full of waste from factories and untreated sewage. Many people died of cholera, a fatal disease spread by a contaminated water supply. In 1859, engineers started constructing an advanced system of brick-built sewers that took the sewage downstream of the city and emptied it into the Thames estuary. Pumping stations like the one above helped at certain places to raise and then push the sewage on through the sewers.

BUILDING TUNNELS

Giant tunneling machines like this one drill or bore road and rail tunnels beneath cities. These machines are fronted by powerful metal teeth that can cut into rock. Behind the cutting edge is a tunneling shield, which protects workers and holds up the tunnel roof and walls as they are excavated. A great danger, especially in areas with soft soil, is from subsidence, or the ground caving in. Shallower tunnels are built by excavating from the surface, a method called cut-and-cover.

Supplying the city

CITIES HAVE ALWAYS DEPENDED on the regions around them for the supply of water, food, and raw materials for manufacturing. In return, cities offered the people of these regions jobs, a chance to trade, and manufactured goods. The area under a city's influence is sometimes called its hinterland, or the "back country." It was by severing the vital links between a city and its hinterland that an invading army could besiege and capture a medieval city. Over the ages, city supply lines have extended over entire nations, continents, and even the whole world. However, it only takes a widespread power failure, a natural disaster, or a war to demonstrate that cities are vulnerable and cannot survive without support from the outside.

SPRING WATER DIRECT
The ancient Romans knew how to bring fresh water from the countryside into their cities. It flowed through long troughs or pipes called aqueducts. When crossing valleys, aqueducts were supported by high arches. In southern France, the Pont du Gard (above) carried water from springs near Uzès to the city of Nemausus (modern-day Nîmes). The 31-mile-(50-km-) long aqueduct was built in the 1st century CE. It supplied the city with water for drinking, public baths, fountains, and waste disposal.

STOCKING UP
Ancient cities stored as many resources as possible within their walls. Granaries kept stocks of grain and cereal, while livestock supplied meat and milk. These provided secure supplies in times of famine or during a siege. Rainwater was stored in cisterns. This magnificent cistern was built under the city of Constantinople (modern Istanbul, Turkey) in the 5th century CE, to supply the Grand Palace. It could hold as much water as 32 modern Olympic-sized swimming pools. This water helped the city survive when besieging armies cut off the supply of water from its aqueducts.

THE BERLIN AIRLIFT
After World War II (1939–45), Germany and its capital city, Berlin, were occupied by the victorious Allied powers—the US, Britain, France, and the Soviet Union (dominated by Russia). Political tensions soon developed between the former allies. In 1948, the Russians cut off the western road and rail links to Berlin so that they alone controlled the city. The US, Britain, and France responded by flying food, fuel, and other supplies into the stricken city. Hundreds of thousands of flights helped the city survive until the Russians lifted the blockade in May 1949.

FOOD FROM OUTSIDE

Cities in remote or harsh landscapes usually get their supplies from far-off regions. This heavily loaded truck is carrying cattle feed into Jaisalmer in the Indian state of Rajasthan. This city is home to more than 60,000 people but lies in a desert region, where there is insufficient water for growing crops, so many people rear cattle for a living. The city depends on more well-watered regions for its essential supplies of food. Cities in fertile regions, or seaports, have easier access to supplies and fewer transportation costs, which helps boost their economy.

Cattle feed carried to market in huge bags

HUNGRY FOR POWER

People in cities use much more electricity than people in rural areas. Las Vegas in Nevada, is famous for its casino resorts that set the desert city alight after dark with their extravagant lighting. The city uses the Hoover Dam on Lake Mead— 30 miles (48 km) south of the city—for both electricity and water supply. How dependent people in cities are upon electricity is shown during power cuts. Electricity from power plants is distributed through grids, and a fault in a grid can lead to blackouts. In 2003, parts of the US and Canada went without power for several hours. The Northeast Blackout, as it was called, affected some 45 million people across eight US states and another 10 million people in Canada.

Bulldozer levels and compacts garbage

WASTEFUL CONSUMPTION

The manufacture and consumption of most things creates waste. Many modern cities have landfill sites on their outskirts, where waste is buried. Waste disposal by burning or burying can pollute the environment and endanger public health. The decomposition of waste releases harmful chemicals such as methane and ammonia, which contaminate the air, soil, and water. Burning releases gases such as nitrogen dioxide, which pollutes the atmosphere, making rain acidic. City governments now encourage citizens to separate waste into glass, paper, wood, and metal, so that they can be recycled.

Running the city

THE FIRST CITIES WERE RULED BY KINGS, who often appointed councils of important people to help them govern. About 2,500 years ago in ancient Greece, the people of Athens chose to be governed instead by an assembly of citizens, who elected (voted in) a city council. Modern cities too have their own councils or assemblies that decide how the city is run. They employ officials to carry out their plans. Councils may be independent from national government and may control their own city police and taxes and have their own budget for housing or education. In democracies, they are made up of representatives elected by local residents. Many private businesses and agencies also work to keep the city running.

COUNCILS AND ELECTIONS
These bronze tokens were used for voting in the *ekklesia* (citizens' assembly) of Athens, before 500 BCE. This was the world's first attempt at a democratic assembly, although women, slaves, and Greeks born in other cities could not be part of it. The everyday running of the city was carried out by an elected council called the *boule*, and citizens were chosen to perform the duties of judges in courts of law.

OFFICERS ON SKATES
Police perform a very important job in our cities by tackling crime and enforcing the law. These Norwegian police officers are using cycles and rollerblades. They can patrol those parts of a city that their police cars cannot easily reach, such as parks or pedestrian areas. Paris had a police force as early as 1667, and Glasgow, Scotland, in 1800. London's Metropolitan Police, founded in 1829, was the model for many other forces around the world.

Tricolor sash worn by an Italian mayor

HEADING THE CITY
Sashes are worn at official events by mayors, or *sindaci*, in Italy. A mayor is the city's leading official, and may be appointed or elected—the system varies from one country to another. He or she may head the city administration and may also act as a kind of ambassador. Mayors may be involved in bidding for the Olympic Games, in encouraging businesses to move to the city, or in twinning—setting up cultural links with other cities around the world.

BRAVE FIREFIGHTERS

These firefighters are tackling a blaze in Oregon. The use of fuels for heating, cooking, or industry in built-up areas means that fire has always been a great danger in cities. From the 1600s, water pumps mounted on horse-drawn wagons were used to put out blazes, and soon after, the first fire departments were formed. Today's firefighters can use the latest breathing apparatuses and fire-resistant clothing, but also have to deal with disasters such as traffic accidents or the spillage of dangerous chemicals.

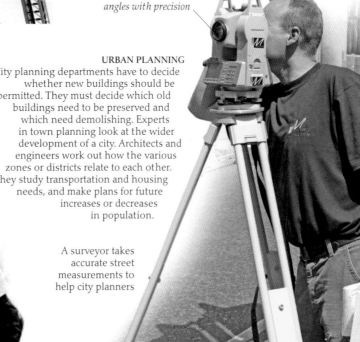

Theodolite measures angles with precision

URBAN PLANNING

City planning departments have to decide whether new buildings should be permitted. They must decide which old buildings need to be preserved and which need demolishing. Experts in town planning look at the wider development of a city. Architects and engineers work out how the various zones or districts relate to each other. They study transportation and housing needs, and make plans for future increases or decreases in population.

A surveyor takes accurate street measurements to help city planners

CLEARING OUT THE GARBAGE

Cities produce huge amounts of waste. New York City produces about 15,500 tons (14,000 metric tons) of garbage every day. Garbage collectors keep the city neat and clean and cart away garbage that can attract vermin or disease. Refuse can be taken to big dumps, buried at landfill sites, or burned in incinerators. All these methods can be harmful to the environment, so more and more of the garbage collected from homes is separated out and recycled, often to make new goods.

Landmarks and symbols

W**HEN PEOPLE THINK OF A CITY,** they often recall a particular image. It may be a well-known building, such as the Sydney Opera House in Australia, or a unique form of transportation, like Venice's gondolas. The popular image could also be a landmark such as Table Mountain, which overlooks Cape Town in South Africa, or a ceremonial uniform like that of the Queen's Guard in London. City symbols form a valuable part of a city's marketing efforts, just like a company's logo. They are often made into souvenirs and appear in travel advertisements. The symbol may even be an idea, such as "Paris in Spring." The Big Apple was just a 1920s nickname for New York until the city's tourism office promoted it 50 years later. Landmarks and symbols are serious business for a city's tourist industry.

St. Basil's Cathedral, Moscow, Russia

LANDMARK NAME

In 1923, an American property developer set up a temporary advertising sign in the Hollywood Hills, near Los Angeles, that read Hollywoodland. With the expansion of the US film industry, and the growing popularity of American films worldwide, this simple sign soon became an international symbol for movies and stardom. In 1949, the sign was changed to read just Hollywood, referring to the city district as a whole.

AMONG MY SOUVENIRS

City icons or symbols are the focus of a thriving trade in cheap souvenirs, both for foreign and domestic tourists. The images may be made into the form of coffee mugs, keyrings, snow globes, or paperweights, and printed on T-shirts, posters, cards, or fridge magnets. Even the most elegant architecture can be represented in brightly colored plastic. Souvenirs are big business, and also help to encourage further tourism. Once they are taken home they act as free advertising, helping to promote the image of a city in other countries.

UNFORGETTABLE!

A tourist poses at the Leaning Tower of Pisa, in Pisa, Italy, making it look as if he is holding up the structure on his own. This famous bell tower was built on poor foundations in 1173, and began to tilt almost immediately. The flaw in its design has made it famous ever since. Other city landmarks may be iconic for their beauty, such as the Shwedagon Pagoda in Yangon, Myanmar, or because they were the sites of important historical events, such as Edinburgh Castle in Scotland. Size and height both make a big impression. A huge statue called *Christ the Redeemer* overlooks Rio de Janeiro in Brazil from a 2,300-ft- (700-m-) high peak, and is a memorable symbol of the vibrant city.

Eiffel Tower, Paris, France

A TICKET TO RIDE

Visitors to a city often remember it because of its transportation. New York City is famous for its yellow cabs, Hong Kong for harbor ferries, and Amsterdam for bicycles. Fantastically decorated minibuses like this one are common in downtown Manila. They are known as jeepneys, as they were originally customized from US army jeeps left behind in the Philippines at the end of World War II in 1945.

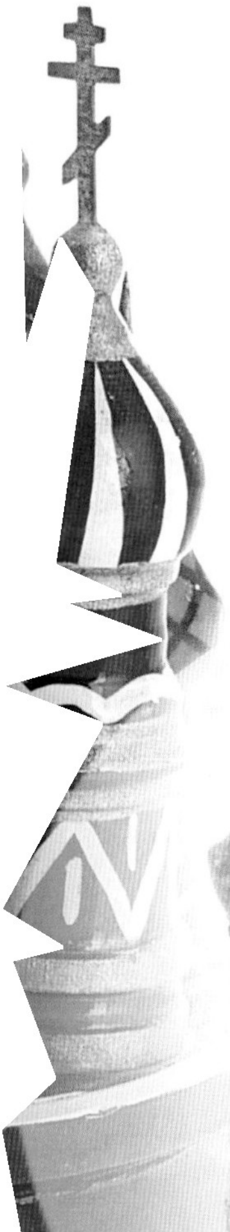

Crown souvenir from
Statue of Liberty, New York City

GIANT WHEELS, LONG VIEWS

A city skyline can be iconic, especially when viewed from a giant revolving wheel. This is the Singapore Flyer, a big wheel that opened in 2008. At 540 ft (165 m) high, it is the world's tallest big wheel, with a view stretching to 28 miles (45 km). Giant wheels themselves can be part of the city skyline. In Austria, Vienna's famous Riesenrad dates back to 1897. The London Eye, erected as recently as 1999, is the UK's most popular paid tourist attraction.

*Sagrada
Familia Church,
Barcelona, Spain*

Barcelona
skyline,
Spain

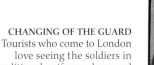

CHANGING OF THE GUARD

Tourists who come to London love seeing the soldiers in traditional uniform who guard the city's palaces. The guards are a historic symbol of the city. The changing of the guard each morning at Buckingham Palace provides a colorful spectacle. Just as famous are the kilt-wearing Evzones of the Presidential Guard in Athens. Military parades and bands form an important part of many state ceremonies, but generally have little impact on the lives of city-dwellers—except for the owners of souvenir stores, who can sell toy soldiers or uniformed dolls.

Open spaces

Today's city-dwellers can find relief from the crowded city by visiting public spaces such as parks, gardens, lakes, and beaches. Cities have always had open spaces, but they have not always been public. Many famous public parks in Europe, such as London's Hyde Park, exist today because they were created in medieval times for the king to hunt deer. From the 17th century onward, gardens such as Tivoli in Copenhagen, Denmark, were created for amusements, such as theater and, later, fairground rides. In the 1930s, city planners began to set aside green belts, or areas where building was restricted. The idea was to prevent cities from swallowing up the countryside and to preserve open spaces on their outer limits.

DIG IT!

City people often live in crowded conditions with little access to fresh air and green spaces. Some are resourceful, however, and a patch of roof can sometimes be turned into a garden. Inner-city gardeners can grow plants in courtyards, alleys, or window-boxes. Living plants can even be used as a roofing material. In Europe, community plots of land are shared among city-dwellers who have no gardens of their own, as places where they can grow their own vegetables.

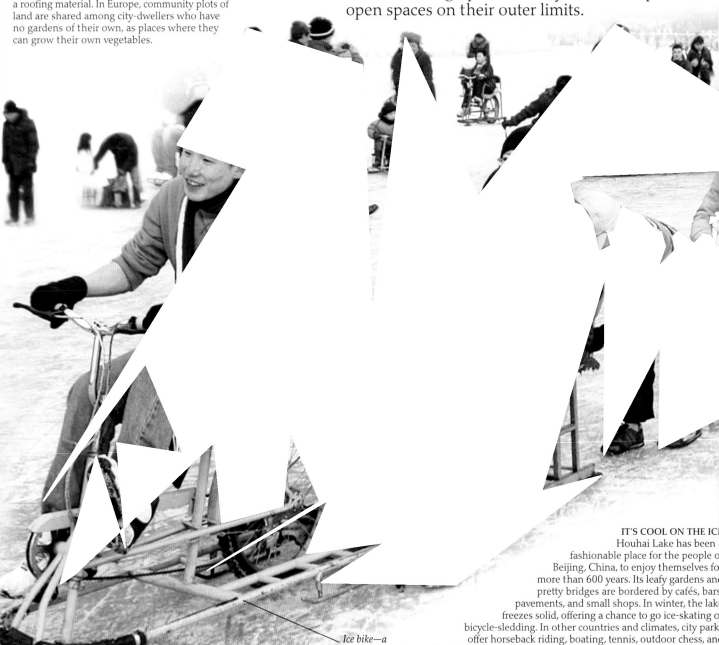

Ice bike—a pedal-powered sled

IT'S COOL ON THE ICE
Houhai Lake has been a fashionable place for the people of Beijing, China, to enjoy themselves for more than 600 years. Its leafy gardens and pretty bridges are bordered by cafés, bars, pavements, and small shops. In winter, the lake freezes solid, offering a chance to go ice-skating or bicycle-sledding. In other countries and climates, city parks offer horseback riding, boating, tennis, outdoor chess, and kite-flying—or simply a chance to walk or jog in a traffic-free zone. Some parks have open-air swimming pools in the heart of the city.

Some big cities are right by the seaside, with golden sands for swimming or surfing. Bondi Beach in Sydney, Waikiki in Honolulu, and Copacabana in Rio de Janeiro are all within easy reach of the city center. What chance do city-dwellers in northern, inland cities have of summer sunbathing? Since 2002, Parisians who cannot reach the sunny south of France in the summer can enjoy Paris Plage—a fake tropical beach beside the Seine River. Beaches with imported sand and palm trees are now present in European cities from Berlin to Budapest.

Chairs have blades welded to the bottom for sit-down skating

Chairs welded together into tandems

A fox scavenges in garbage cans in London

A PARK IS A PARADISE
The word paradise originally meant a walled garden or park. To urban New Yorkers, Manhattan's Central Park is a heaven of its own. Amid the clamor of the downtown streets, the park is a peaceful strip of grass, trees, rockeries, pathways, and ponds, with children's playgrounds and entertainments. The park attracts 25 million visitors a year. Parks occupy some of the most valuable land in any city, but to city planners they are worth far more as green spaces than as building sites.

CITY WILDLIFE
Surprisingly, cities, with their parks and wasteland, are often havens for wildlife. Cities are generally warmer than the surrounding countryside and have fewer predators. Huge flocks of pigeons fill many squares. In Australia, urban species include cockatoos and possums; in Africa and India, vultures and kites; in North America, raccoons; and in Europe, foxes and squirrels. The availability of food among trash generated in the cities attracts these animals.

Metropolitan arts

CITIES ARE POWERHOUSES OF THE ARTS. Many artists and musicians are inspired by city life, and it is here too that they find their largest audiences. The larger the city, the greater the diversity of theaters, opera houses, and concert halls, as well as art galleries, museums, and arts festivals. A lively arts scene can play a part in bringing new life to run-down quarters of cities and can boost the local economy. Cities often host splendid exhibitions or grand concerts, but some of the most exciting artistic expression is informal and unofficial. It may take the form of graffiti art, carnival costume, or any kind of popular music, dance, or theater seen on the streets.

ARTISTIC VISION
The Guggenheim Museum in the Basque city of Bilbao, Spain, has been exhibiting modern art since it opened in 1997. It also stands as a great work of art in its own right. The museum was designed by the North American architect Frank Gehry and is built of stone and glass sheathed in titanium. This fascinating building has attracted more than 10 million visitors to Bilbao and marks out the city as a center of culture and innovation.

Angel with the Sponge by Antonio Giorgetti (died 1670)

THUMP THAT BASS!
Live music can add a cheerful or nostalgic mood to a city center. This double-bass player is performing on the pavement in Santiago de Cuba, Cuba's second-largest city. Buskers, who play or sing in return for a few coins given by passers-by, or to raise funds for a charity, choose city centers where they will attract the greatest number of people. Underground tunnels or subways can provide natural amplification and echo.

POTAVERVNT
ME ACETO

STONE ANGEL
This statue of an angel stands guard on a bridge in Rome called the Ponte Sant'Angelo. Early cities were often decorated with public statues of gods or mythical figures. From the 1600s, public squares, fountains, and palaces in Europe were adorned with statues of kings and queens, soldiers on horseback, saints, and heroes. During the 20th century, public art has come to include statues of ordinary people too, and fantastic abstract designs or installations.

GRAFFITI ART

Graffiti are words or pictures drawn on walls in public places. They are nothing new, because they were being scrawled on walls in the Roman city of Pompeii in 79 CE. The owners of the walls do not often welcome graffiti, and criminal gangs may use it as a threatening territory sign. However, about 30 years ago teenagers were creating such inventive graffiti that these began to be accepted as art. Otavio and Gustavo Pandolfo, known as Os Gemêos ("the Twins") became famous for their graffiti in São Paulo, Brazil. They are now invited to paint on walls in cities around the world.

B-boy in
New York City

CITIES OF CULTURE

In Russia, St. Petersburg is famous for its ballet, and in Italy, Milan is linked to the opera. Beijing, the Chinese capital, gives its name to a very different type of opera. This was first performed at Beijing's imperial court in 1790, although its roots can be found in other Chinese regions. Beijing opera generally tells fantastic tales of folklore, of heroes, villains, and lovers. The story is told through dance and movement, speech, song, and music, and is colorful but never realistic.

Toukui
(opera headdress)

An actor in the role of Qing Yi,
*one of the main female
characters in Beijing opera*

DANCING IN THE STREETS

This acrobatic type of street dance developed along with early hip-hop music in New York City in the late 1970s. Known as breakdancing, breaking, or b-boying, it soon spread around the world's cities. Street dance has a long history. New crazes have often begun in poorer areas of a city, in slums or shanty towns. Nearly 100 years earlier, Rio de Janeiro in Brazil produced the samba, while the people of Buenos Aires, Argentina, shocked polite society with the tango.

Beijing opera

Mayan ball player

Sporting life

WHEN THE ANCIENT ROMANS visited their public baths, they often used the exercise area for a workout with weights or for a ball game. Every Aztec city had a stone ball-court, laid out according to religious rules. Their high-speed game, called *tlachtli*, was like a cross between baseball and volleyball, and some noblemen would bet all their wealth on the outcome. In modern times, watching and playing sports remains an urban obsession. Many cities' names are forever linked with their sports teams—the Boston Red Sox for baseball, Manchester United or Real Madrid for soccer, or the Toronto Maple Leafs for ice hockey. A sports stadium or arena may be an iconic part of a city's history, such as the Melbourne Cricket Ground (MCG) in Australia.

ANCIENT GAMES
Spectator sports and races were an essential part of life in ancient cities. Two thousand years ago, the Circus Maximus, a chariot-racing stadium in Rome, could hold 250,000 spectators. In Central American cities, ritual ball games were played for hundreds of years. The Mayan version of the game, called *pitz*, was literally a matter of life and death—a team might be killed for losing. Players wore heavy body padding, shown above, to deflect the hard rubber ball, which weighed as much as 9 lb (4 kg).

Arc de Triomphe, Paris

CITY TEAMS
In medieval Europe, people played chaotic ball games, loosely called "football," and this developed into different sports in different countries. In 1863, England's Football Association drew up the rules of association football, or soccer. This produced a new game popular in industrial cities, such as Birmingham and Liverpool, and soon all over the world. Many of today's biggest clubs are still based in industrial cities, where crowds of fiercely loyal supporters pack into giant stadiums. Santos FC, pictured in white, is a club based in Santos, a Brazilian port city. The legendary player Pelé played for the club in 1956 to 1974.

THE BIG RUN
Tens of thousands of people take part each year in running events called marathons. These take their name from a run supposed to have been made in Greece in 490 BCE, all the way from the battlefield of Marathon to Athens. The distance is 26 miles, 385 yards (42.195 km). Big events, passing city-center landmarks, include those in New York, Paris, and London. In the Paris marathon, runners follow a route that takes them past city landmarks such as the Eiffel Tower, the Arc de Triomphe, and Notre Dame Cathedral. Marathons are run by serious athletes as well as by amateurs who just want to prove they can cover the distance.

OLYMPIC CITIES
The city-states of ancient Greece held great athletics contests dedicated to the gods. The ancient Olympic Games were held from at least 776 BCE until 393 CE. The games were revived in 1894, and since then have been held in a different world city every four years. For the athletes, the Olympics offer a chance to compete against the best in the world's biggest sporting event. For the cities, they are an opportunity to develop tourism and create new sporting arenas. And for fans like these Australian supporters at the 2000 Sydney Olympics, they offer a chance to witness the finest in sport and support representatives of their own country

GETTING FROM A TO B

Some sports, such as parkour and freerunning, are practiced only in cities. Parkour, a noncompetitive sport that originated in the 1980s in some French cities, involves negotiating the obstacles along a given route in a city by the most efficient and fluid movements of the body. It includes simple motions such as running, climbing over walls, jumping, vaulting, or crawling. Freerunning is a more acrobatic and showy version of parkour. Both sports develop strength, speed, and balance, while making use of the city's natural obstacle courses. They are now popular in cities all over the world.

MEAN STREETS

Some city names, from Indianopolis to Le Mans, will always be associated with car racing because of their famous tracks. The Monaco Grand Prix, one of several races on the Formula 1 (F1) circuit, dates back to 1929. It actually takes place on the city streets of Monte Carlo, which are closed for the duration of the race. The narrow circuit was never designed for F1 racing. It borders a famous harbor beside the Mediterranean Sea, and includes tight corners and a road tunnel, making it one of the most challenging Grand Prix circuits in the world.

A parkour side vault

Festival!

PEOPLE IN VILLAGES AND TOWNS celebrate festivals, but it is in cities where the concentration of life leads to unique festivities. Some city festivals are now famous worldwide, such as the Mardi Gras—the carnival in New Orleans in Louisiana. It is celebrated by both residents and tourists. Many festivals have religious origins—the word holiday comes from "holy day." In ancient Babylon the spring festival of Akitu was a 12-day public celebration with music and singing. In ancient Rome, the winter festival of Saturnalia honored the god Saturn. In the Christian cities of medieval Europe saints' days and Holy Week were marked by holidays and processions. Many festivals developed non-religious aspects. They became a chance for people of all classes to relax and escape from social convention and the pressures of city life.

MASKED IN VENICE
Carnival means "farewell to meat." It was originally an occasion of feasting before the annual Christian fast of Lent, when no meat could be eaten for 40 days. Carnival became a time for dancing. People wore masks at ball (parties), concealing their true identity and social class. The Italian city of Venice traditionally had the most elegant masks (above). Thousands of masked revelers still visit Venice during the carnival.

PARADING IN RIO
Perhaps the most famous of all carnival cities is Rio de Janeiro, Brazil. The revelry here dates back to the 1720s and today it takes the form of a vast carnival parade, which throbs to the rhythm of samba music. Many of the people taking part belong to rival samba schools, who parade in outrageous costumes and headdresses. This float (moving platform) is decked out as a ship and is accompanied by "swimmers."

GANESH CHATURTHI
This 10-day Hindu religious festival that usually starts in August honors the god Ganesh, the elephant-headed son of Shiva and Parvati. People pray and make offerings before statues of Ganesh, and cook sweet dumplings called *modak* to mark the occasion. The festival ends with the statues being immersed in a river or the seashore. While the festival is celebrated in different parts of India, it is particularly popular in Mumbai (above).

SIGHTS OF SEVILLE
The *feria*, or fair, of Seville, the capital of Spain's Andalucia region, takes place on the west bank of the Guadalquivir River each April. For a week, a cavalcade of riders and carriages passes by, with local families in traditional costume—broad-brimmed hats for the men, frilled dresses in brilliant colors for the ladies. Pavilions called *casetas* are erected for the fiery dancing, singing, and guitar music known as flamenco.

Women dancing in traditional flamenco dress

GREEN FOR ST. PATRICK
National days are often celebrated with parades and marching bands. The Republic of Ireland honors its patron, St. Patrick (c. 387–461 CE), with a festival held each year on March 17. Cities overseas with large populations of Irish descent celebrate it with even more enthusiasm. In the US, up to 2 million people line the streets of New York City to watch the St. Patrick's Day parade. In Chicago, even the river is dyed green, the national color of Ireland.

Reveler on float wearing a spectacular costume

The float of the Vila Isabel samba school enters the Sambadrome parade ground in Rio de Janeiro

Tower of sweet steamed buns on bamboo frame

Contestant gathering buns

LUCKY BUNS
Cheung Chau is an island in Hong Kong. Each year, usually early in May, the god of the sea, Pak Tai—who people say once saved the island from a plague—is honored with a festival. For three days, no one eats meat. The streets shake to the sound of drums and gongs and children in fine costumes are held up on high metal poles above a parade. At midnight, young men scramble up tall towers of steamed buns. As they snatch the buns from the tower, those who get the highest buns win good fortune for their families in the coming year.

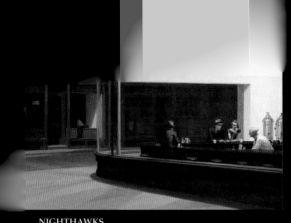

...y never sleeps

BIG CITIES NEVER REALLY SHUT DOWN. Unlike smaller towns, they stay active 24 hours a day and seven days a week. Most cities have districts where clubs, theaters, and restaurants open late into the night, and where people go for entertainment or a bite to eat. These areas, such as London's West End, the French Quarter of New Orleans, and Ginza in Tokyo, also attract tourists and people from out of town. In contrast, the business districts of cities may seem deserted at night. But even here people still go about their work, cleaning underground stations, guarding building sites, and staffing hotel desks. Many factories keep production running continuously, with the working day divided into sections called shifts.

NIGHTHAWKS
The American artist Edward Hopper named his famous 1942 painting *Nighthawks*—a word for city-dwellers who stay out late at night. *Nighthawks* shows a corner cafe in Greenwich Village, a district of New York City. It is late at night and there are just three customers left inside. The lighting is harsh, and the streets outside are empty. The painting shows how city life can be bleak and lonely, especially once the daytime crowds have gone home.

THE BUZZ
Loud music and a spectacular light show generate excitement among clubbers in the city of Birmingham, England. Nightclubs, concert venues, theaters, movie theaters, and restaurants all create a buzz in a city. Cities thrive on a reputation for fun, since a booming entertainment industry attracts people to come and spend money, creating jobs and income. Most cities have laws regulating the entertainment sector. Strict religious rules in Dubai, United Arab Emirates, ban dancing and loud music in outdoor places, and many other cities determine venue closing times. Sometimes curfews are imposed in cities to maintain public order, forcing people to return to their homes before a certain time every day, silencing the city's nightlife.

Official sign distinguishes taxi cabs

THE NIGHTSHIFT
Taxis line up at a taxi stand in Istanbul, Turkey. After public transportation services such as buses and trams close down late at night, large cities are filled with taxis, which ferry home shift workers, partygoers, and other night owls. Office cleaners, security guards, factory workers, call center staff, hospital nurses, doctors, and many others may have to work a nightshift. Workers get used to working odd hours, but this can interrupt natural sleep patterns and interfere with the routines of family life.

A GHASTLY GLARE

The first city streets to be lit by electricity were in Paris and London in the 1870s. Lighting made streets and sidewalks safer for people, helping them find their way in the dark. Today's cities are brighter than ever, with electric light coming from homes, offices, car headlights, and advertising signs. In this picture, an orange glare fills the night sky above Shanghai in China. It is created mainly by inefficient, nondirectional streetlights, which shine up into the sky just as much as downward to the street. Too much light is a type of pollution, since it disrupts and disorientates songbirds, night-flying insects, and other wildlife and makes it difficult for people to see the stars. This is why most astronomical observatories are far from cities. Light pollution is also thought to affect people's health by interfering with their sleep cycles.

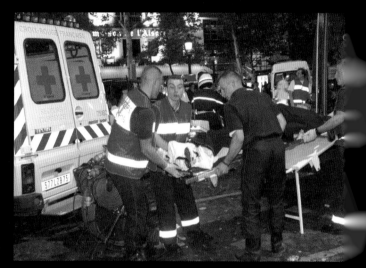

EMERGENCY CALL

Nighttime emergencies happen everywhere, but in a city, where streets remain busy around the clock, accidents are frequent at night. This ambulance crew is dealing with a late-night emergency on the streets of Paris. Accidents are more frequent still during festive periods when people party until morning. In the Scottish cities of Edinburgh and Glasgow, the most ambulance calls happen between two and four in the morning on New Year's Eve, during Hogmanay celebrations. Other emergency services must also be on standby, ready to fight a fire or investigate a crime.

SHOP AROUND THE CLOCK

More and more city corner stores and supermarkets are open around the clock. They are convenient for people who are unable to shop by day, or might want to buy a sandwich at three in the morning. However, national or city trading laws may regulate opening hours to limit nighttime disturbance to nearby residents, or so that religious customs are observed.

Battling the elements

Openings in tower catch the breeze

CITIES MAY BE BUILT HIGH in the mountains, or on low-lying islands. They may lie in the steamy tropics, or in the icy lands above the Arctic Circle. Cities may experience extreme climates, seasonal rains or floods, dust storms, tornadoes, heavy snowfall, or great heat. These challenges can be met by providing shelters in tornado-prone areas, constructing earthquake-resistant buildings, and strengthening flood defenses. Architecture must suit the climate, with pitched (sloping) roofs and gutters provided for rain, reinforced roofs for heavy snow, and shutters and awnings for the heat. A city's climate influences how people live and dress, even when and how they work. In Spanish cities, for example, where the afternoon Sun is hot, people stop work for a midday nap, or siesta.

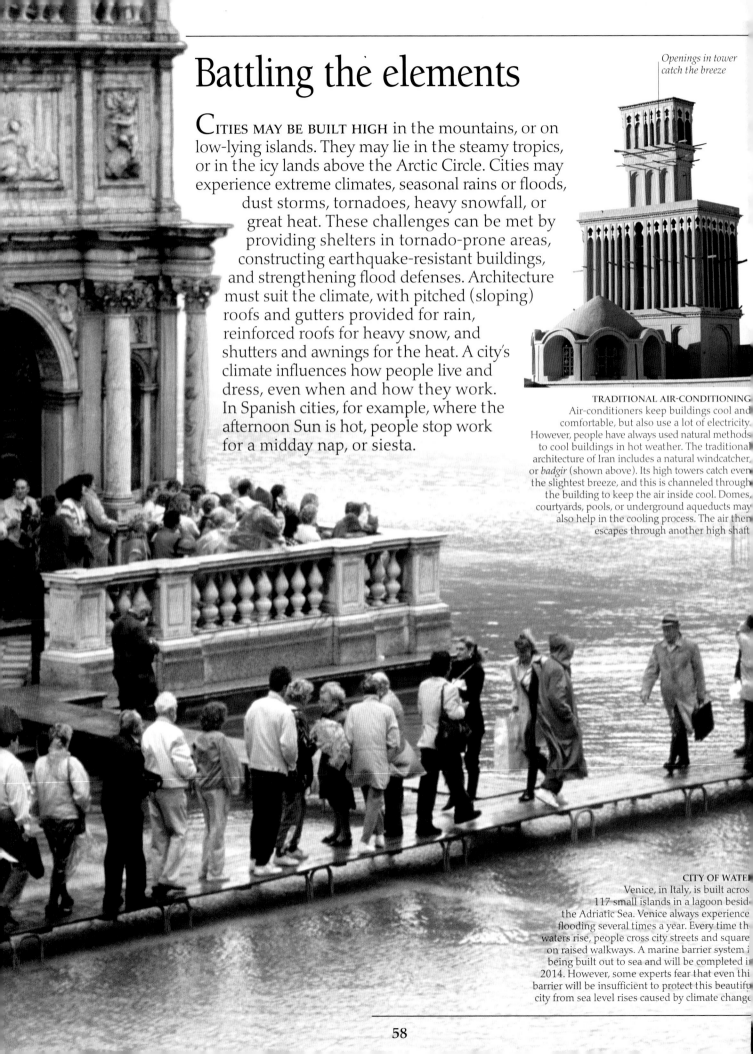

TRADITIONAL AIR-CONDITIONING
Air-conditioners keep buildings cool and comfortable, but also use a lot of electricity. However, people have always used natural methods to cool buildings in hot weather. The traditional architecture of Iran includes a natural windcatcher, or *badgir* (shown above). Its high towers catch even the slightest breeze, and this is channeled through the building to keep the air inside cool. Domes, courtyards, pools, or underground aqueducts may also help in the cooling process. The air then escapes through another high shaft

CITY OF WATER
Venice, in Italy, is built across 117 small islands in a lagoon beside the Adriatic Sea. Venice always experiences flooding several times a year. Every time the waters rise, people cross city streets and squares on raised walkways. A marine barrier system is being built out to sea and will be completed in 2014. However, some experts fear that even this barrier will be insufficient to protect this beautiful city from sea level rises caused by climate change

CLEARING THE SNOW

Ottawa, the capital of Canada, has hot summers, where the temperature can reach 86°F (30°C). In contrast, during the long, cold winter it can drop as low as –22°F (–30°C). The snow cover may last for up to four months of the year. Snow plows with blowers attached clear heavy snow drifts from roads and sidewalks by loading the snow into trucks. Insulated buildings and pipes prevent heat loss and freezing. During the winter, people also enjoy skating on the city's Rideau Canal.

THE HIGH LIFE

El Alto (Spanish for "the heights") is a district of La Paz, the capital of Bolivia. At its highest point, El Alto reaches 13,615 feet (4,150 m). The shortage of oxygen in the air in high-altitude cities can affect the human body. The 2.3 million citizens of La Paz have, however, become used to such conditions, like these women sitting by a road in El Alto. Their bodies have adapted to take in more oxygen from the thin air of the Andes mountains. But visitors who are not acclimatized may at first experience dizziness, headaches, and nausea—a condition known as altitude sickness.

CHOKING ON SMOKE

The natural environment can combine with artificial pollution to affect city life. Smog is created when chemicals from traffic exhaust and factories react with sunlight. It is at its worst in low-lying regions where there are few winds to disperse the particles. Smog reduces visibility and can cause severe breathing difficulties, cancers, and other diseases. When smog conditions get really bad, city-dwellers, like this woman in Beijing, wear masks to protect themselves.

RIVER CITY

The city of Iquitos in Peru is connected to the outside world only by riverboat and aircraft, not by road transportation. It is deep in the Amazon Rainforest, about 1,865 miles (3,000 km) inland from the Atlantic Ocean. The climate is warm and humid, and suitable for growing rubber—the reason for the city's growth over the past 100 years. The city depends on boats and ferries to bring in its supplies. There are heavy rains from December to May, but during the dry season the level of the river may go down by 40 ft (12 m), making it difficult for supply boats to come upstream.

In the danger zone

THE FIRST CITIES WERE BUILT TO PROVIDE secure homes. Even so, people have often set up cities in places of extreme danger. Many urban areas occupy earthquake zones. A major fault line in the Earth's crust runs through the state of California. In 1906, over 3,000 people died when an earthquake destroyed the city of San Francisco, triggering fires from broken gas mains. Some cities are built within range of volcanoes, which may erupt at any time. Ports may be regularly battered by hurricanes or overwhelmed by floods. In every case, the population believes the advantages of city life outweigh potential dangers. The best land or the best harbor may seem to people to be worth a high-risk location.

FIRE HAZARDS
Sometimes city disasters are not caused by the forces of nature, but by the way cities are built. In old cities, thatched roofs, timber housing, and narrow streets meant that a blaze could quickly get out of control. In 1666, a five-day fire in London (above) destroyed 13,200 houses, 89 churches, and a cathedral. Today, fireproof building materials and fire services can prevent or limit damage.

Mask contains pungent herbs as a defense against plague

Waxed robes were thought to be a barrier to disease

DISEASE AND PLAGUE
Plagues spread by rat fleas killed thousands across Asia and Europe from the 1300s to the 1700s. Venice, an important port in the 16th century, was particularly affected as ships laden with silks and spices also brought in the disease. In 1577, nearly 50,000 died of the plague, which spread due to insanitary living conditions and dense housing. Doctors tried to protect ____ dressing in robes and

THE GREAT QUAKE
It is very hard to predict when earthquakes will occur. The Great Hanshin Earthquake of 1995 killed 6,434 people and caused nearly $103 billion worth of damage. Centered near the port city of Kobe, Japan, the earthquake even destroyed an elevated highway. With the help of technology, civil engineers can design buildings strong enough to withstand shocks, but in poorer regions, where housing is less robust, the loss of life may be horrific.

GOING VOLCANIC!
When the Italian volcano Mount Vesuvius, near the city of Naples, erupted in 79 CE, it destroyed the cities of Pompeii and Herculaneum. The volcano has erupted on about 40 other occasions, the last time in 1944. Volcanic soils are often very fertile, and that is why people have continued to settle in this dangerous region. The population of the Bay of Naples has grown rapidly since 1944, and the regional government is trying to persuade people to move away from the areas most at risk. If Vesuvius erupts again, 600,000 people may have to be evacuated at short notice.

Volcanic cloud of ash and stones above the Bay of Naples, 1944

Framed family portrait rescued from flooded house in New Orleans

WHEN THE LEVEES BROKE

New Orleans, Louisiana, has a population of nearly 1.2 million. Built beside the Mississippi River, the city is situated below sea level and directly in the path of seasonal hurricanes. High earthen banks called levees protect it from flooding. In 2005, Hurricane Katrina swept over the region, and the strong winds caused a storm surge, raising the sea level. The surge, nearly 30 ft (9 m) high, breached the levees, flooding New Orleans. A million people fled the city, but as the muddy flood waters engulfed homes, many people who stayed back were drowned or left clinging to their rooftops. Vast areas of the region were left without power. Katrina killed a total of 1,836 people.

NUCLEAR DISASTER

Sometimes, cities are built near hazardous industries to provide a workforce, but this exposes the people to the possibility of harm caused by industrial accidents. The town of Pripyat near the city of Chernobyl, in Ukraine (then part of the Soviet Union), housed people needed to work at the local nuclear power plant. When one of the plant's reactors exploded in 1986, deadly clouds of radiation escaped. In addition to the workers who died immediately, thousands died from cancers in the following years. About 800,000 children in the region were exposed to the radiation. The town was immediately abandoned.

Chernobyl nuclear pl

Cities of the future

Cabin can rotate
through 360 degrees

Cities will continue to grow in the 21st century. Urbanization is expected to peak in around 2100, by which time three-quarters of the world's people could be living in cities. This will occur as long as cities are promising places to live, with jobs and a good quality of life. There are, however, many unknown factors. Growing cities might not thrive in a period of climate change, floods, and droughts. Shortages of food, water, and resources such as oil are predicted as the world's population grows. This could lead to social unrest and conflict, even war. The future of the world's cities will depend not just on new technologies, but also on our ability to adapt and plan for change.

Singapore dollars

NEW CITY-STATES?

Today's global cities, such as London, New York, and Hong Kong, often have as much in common with each other as they do with the nations of which they are a part. Similarities between cities are encouraged by a global economy, instant communication, and multicultural populations. Singapore is an island city-state that is truly global. It has a population of 5 million people, including Chinese, Malays, Indians, and Europeans, and a fast-growing international-based economy. There could well be more city-states like Singapore in the future.

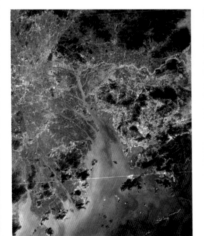

MEGA-REGIONS

Urbanization is not just a process of people from rural areas moving into cities. More and more cities will spread out into the countryside, engulfing small towns and villages. Already, mega-cities are merging into huge, urbanized mega-regions. This view of the south China coast takes in the cities of Shenzhen, Guangzhou, and Hong Kong, and the entire interconnected urban area has a population of more than 100 million.

DEATH OF THE CITY

For some people, it is no longer necessary to commute into cities to work. Email, broadband internet, and video conferencing make it possible for people to work from home, from rural areas, or from hotels while on vacation. This electronic revolution will allow people to live wherever they want in the future, even in quiet, remote areas, and cities may one day become redundant.

WE NEED WATER

The rapid pace of urbanization has put tremendous pressure on scarce resources. Many cities such as Chennai (formerly Madras), in Tamil Nadu, India, already face severe water shortage. Chennai depends on collecting and storing water from the annual monsoon. It is also building desalination plants, which remove the salt from sea water. If urbanization continues at this pace or accelerates, coping with limited resources will be a challenge for cities.

TRANSPORTATION OF THE FUTURE?
The popular science-fiction comics of the 1950s showed people zooming around cities using personal jet-packs by the year 2000, but that never happened. What does the future really hold for city transportation? This is the Pivo 2 electric car, dreamed up by engineers at the Japanese car manufacturer Nissan for use in crowded, polluted cities. It can drive sideways or forward as the driver wishes. It runs entirely on electricity and has zero emissions, unlike gas and diesel engines, whose exhaust causes asthma, bronchitis, and allergies. Electric cars still have to win a place in the market, but future transportation, whatever its design, must not burn fossil fuels.

Wheel can pivot through 90 degrees to drive vehicle sideways

FICTIONAL FUTURE
For thousands of years writers and thinkers have liked to dream of ideal cities, the homes of gods or heroes, or triumphs of human technology and achievement. Others have had a darker idea of cities, showing them as bleak, corrupt, industrial landscapes where humanity loses its soul. Science-fiction writers have imagined both possibilities for the future. In the famous German film *Metropolis* (1927), director Fritz Lang portrayed a futuristic mega-city where workers toiled in merciless underground factories, while a small elite enjoyed riches and bright lights in luxury skyscrapers.

Poster for the film *Metropolis*

Building mimics natural shapes

GREEN CITY
Planners and architects try to use technology to create better designs for the future. This is a planned self-sufficient city to be built among the hills and lakes south of Seoul, the capital of South Korea. The site will offer high-density housing for 77,000 people, plus office space, storess, auditoriums, schools, and parking. The circular buildings are designed with terraces equipped with a floor-to-floor circulation system that will store water for irrigating plants. In the future, new cities might look similar to this.

Gwanggyo Power Center project, Seoul, South Korea

Landscaped to look like adjoining park land

Void provides for light and ventilation

Ring is larger than the one above, giving this floor a terrace for outdoor life

Top 10 cities

Best-connected cities

The business world needs to know which are the best cities so that companies can decide where to locate their offices and operations. Every year, the firm Mercer makes a Quality of Living Survey of cities, scoring them on their quality of life, environmental impact, and infrastructure. This list shows Mercer's 2009 rankings for infrastructure, or how well-connected cities are in terms of transportation, electricity and water supply, and communication links. Maintaining infrastructure is expensive, so listed cities tend to be in wealthier countries.

Yokohama and Minato Minai Harbor, Japan

1. SINGAPORE
2. MUNICH, GERMANY
3. COPENHAGEN, DENMARK
4. TSUKUBA, JAPAN
5. YOKOHAMA, JAPAN

= 6. DÜSSELDORF, GERMANY
= 6. VANCOUVER, CANADA
= 8. FRANKFURT, GERMANY
= 8. HONG KONG, CHINA
= 8. LONDON, UK

Sky Train, Vancouver

Best cities to live in

Just what is it that makes a city an enjoyable or pleasant place to live? Excitement, fashion, or atmosphere cannot be measured. Mercer's annual survey is based on 39 criteria, such as political stability and cost of living, as well as the quality of facilities for recreation, housing, medical care, and education. The top US city is Honolulu, Hawaii, at rank 31. The top UK city is London, at rank 39. Cities tied on the same score are given equal rank.

1. VIENNA, AUSTRIA
2. ZURICH, SWITZERLAND
3. GENEVA, SWITZERLAND
= 4. VANCOUVER, CANADA
= 4. AUCKLAND, NEW ZEALAND
6. DÜSSELDORF, GERMANY
= 7. FRANKFURT, GERMANY
= 7. MUNICH, GERMANY
9. BERN, SWITZERLAND
10. SYDNEY, AUSTRALIA

Shoppers in central Vienna

Seaside Auckland, the "city of sails"

The greenest cities

City planners need to monitor the impact on the environment while planning their projects. Mercer's 2010 survey takes into account factors such as availability of clean drinking water, quality of sewage disposal systems, and traffic congestion, to list the top "eco-cities." The survey rates cities according to how much they use energy from sources such as the Sun, wind, and ocean tides, since these can be naturally renewed. It also measures the level of air and noise pollution. Cities tied on the same score are given equal rank.

An urban neighborhood in Helsinki

1. CALGARY, CANADA
2. HONOLULU
= 3. OTTAWA, CANADA
= 3. HELSINKI, FINLAND
5. WELLINGTON, NEW ZEALAND

6. MINNEAPOLIS
7. ADELAIDE, AUSTRALIA
8. COPENHAGEN, DENMARK
= 9. KOBE, JAPAN
= 9. OSLO, NORWAY

Most expensive cities

Which are the world's most expensive cities? The firm ECA International makes an annual survey of cities to find out the cost of living for visitors. The survey focuses on the price of daily needs, such as food, clothing, and entertainment. This 2010 list is made up mainly of cities in the world's wealthiest countries. It might be surprising that Luanda is ranked third, but that is because Angola's oil reserves have brought foreign investors to the city, and it is very expensive to maintain their luxury lifestyle in this war-torn country.

1. TOKYO, JAPAN

2. OSLO, NORWAY

3. LUANDA, ANGOLA

4. NAGOYA, JAPAN

5. YOKOHAMA, JAPAN

6. STAVANGER, NORWAY

7. KOBE, JAPAN

8. COPENHAGEN, DENMARK

9. GENEVA, SWITZERLAND

10. ZURICH, SWITZERLAND

People shopping at a supermarket in Tokyo

Most populous cities

These are the 10 most populated urban areas in the world. The statistics are based on areas of continuously built-up land, as shown by mapping and satellite images. The rankings reflect rapid urbanization as people move from countryside to city, and also the process of conurbation (see pages 30–31), with cities growing and merging with others in the region. Seven of the top 10 cities are in Asia, and the other three in the Americas.

1. TOKYO-YOKOHAMA, JAPAN (35.2 MILLION)

2. JAKARTA, INDONESIA (22)

3. MUMBAI, INDIA (21.25)

4. DELHI, INDIA (20.99)

5. MANILA, PHILIPPINES (20.79)

6. NEW YORK CITY (20.61)

7. SÃO PAULO, BRAZIL (20.18)

8. SEOUL-INCHEON, SOUTH KOREA (19.91)

9. MEXICO CITY, MEXICO (18.69)

10. SHANGHAI, CHINA (18.4)

(All figures are in millions)

A crowded pavement in São Paulo

Highest capital cities

Some cities are built high above sea level, in mountain ranges or highlands, or on plateaus (high plains). These areas may be settled because of their strategic location. La Paz, for instance, lay on the gold and silver trading route to the west coast of South America. This list includes national capitals, but not cities classed as regional capitals, such as Lhasa, capital of Tibet (altitude 11,450 ft/3,490 m).

1. LA PAZ, BOLIVIA 11,910 FT (3,630 M)

2. QUITO, ECUADOR 9,249 FT (2,819 M)

3. THIMPHU, BHUTAN 8,976 FT (2,736 M)

4. BOGOTÁ, COLOMBIA 8,675 FT (2,644 M)

5. ADDIS ABABA, ETHIOPIA 7,900 FT (2,408 M)

6. ASMARA, ERITREA 7,789 FT (2,374 M)

7. SANA'A, YEMEN 7,392 FT (2,253 M)

8. MEXICO CITY, MEXICO 7,270 FT (2,216 M)

9. KABUL, AFGHANISTAN 5,928 FT (1,807 M)

10. NAIROBI, KENYA 5,670 FT (1,728 M)

Trashi Chhoe Dzong, the seat of the Bhutanese government, in Thimphu

Sights and monuments

CITIES ARE IDENTIFIED BY their famous buildings and monuments. These are useful landmarks for the visitor, and may be used as icons by city councils or by advertisers who wish to promote the city. They offer fascinating glimpses of the city at various points in its history. Many of them, such as the pyramids of Giza, are important archeological sites or have religious or symbolic significance. Some, such as the Opera House in Sydney, are more important for their architecture or function in the city.

STATUE OF LIBERTY, NEW YORK, 1886
A symbol of freedom, the 305-ft (93-m) statue was given to the US, on its 100th birthday, by France.

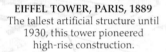

EIFFEL TOWER, PARIS, 1889
The tallest artificial structure until 1930, this tower pioneered high-rise construction.

BRANDENBURG GATE, BERLIN, 1791
This former city gate, built in a style influenced by ancient Greek architecture, is today the symbol of a unified Berlin and Germany.

COLOSSEUM, ROME, 80 CE
Constructed on the orders of emperor Titus, this amphitheater of ancient Rome was the scene of bloody combat by gladiators.

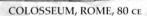

PARTHENON, ATHENS, 438 BCE
This temple and treasury dedicated to the ancient Greek goddess Athena, stands on the Acropolis, a great natural rock platform above the Greek capital.

BLUE MOSQUE, ISTANBUL, 1616
The Sultan Ahmet Mosque, with its graceful minarets and domes, is also known as the Blue Mosque, because of the blue tiles in its interior.

GOLDEN TEMPLE, AMRITSAR, 1586–1604
The center of the Sikh faith, this temple is situated in the middle of an artificial lake.

TIANTAN, BEIJING, 1406–20
The beautiful Temple of Heaven is at the center of a Taoist religious site in the Chinese capital.

MERLION, SINGAPORE, 1964
A modern tourism logo, this half-fish, half-lion statue has become a popular icon of the city-state.

PALACIO DE BELLAS ARTES, MEXICO CITY, 1904–34
Famous center of theater, ballet, and art.

CHRIST THE REDEEMER, RIO DE JANEIRO, 1921–31
This 130-ft- (40-m-) high statue is set on a peak overlooking the Brazilian city.

BIG BEN, LONDON, 1859
The clock tower of the Houses of Parliament of the UK is commonly known, a little inaccurately, by the name of its bell.

SAINT BASIL'S CATHEDRAL, MOSCOW, 1555–61,
A splendid onion-domed cathedral of the Russian Orthodox Church, in the capital's Red Square.

THE FOUNDERS, KIEV, 1982
According to a legend, three brothers and a sister sailed across the Dnieper River and founded what is now the Ukrainian capital.

DOME OF THE ROCK, JERUSALEM, 691–692 CE
Also called Masjid Qubbat As-Sakhrah, one of the holiest shrines in Islam.

THE PYRAMIDS, GIZA, c. 2558–2532 BCE
The Great Sphinx stands before the massive Pyramid of Khafre at Giza, burial site of the Egyptian pharaohs.

BURJ AL-ARAB, DUBAI, 1994
This 1,053-ft- (321-m-) high hotel was built to look like the sail of a traditional Arab dhow, or ship.

TODAI-JI TEMPLE, NARA, 728 CE
The world's largest wooden building is part of a Japanese Buddhist temple complex.

OPERA HOUSE, SYDNEY, 1973
This center for the performing arts beside Sydney Harbour is one of the most famous pieces of architecture in the world.

CN TOWER, TORONTO, 1973–76
This broadcasting tower was the tallest in the world until 2007, when Burj Khalifa, Dubai, surpassed it.

Cities by numbers

Today's CITIES ARE LARGER, busier, and richer than ever before. Their high-rise buildings tower up to a third of a mile (half a kilometer) or more above their streets. We know this because many experts and companies are interested in data on cities. They need figures on population numbers and density, building and development, economics, transportation, crime, and many other aspects of city life. Historians study these data to see how cities have changed over time. Town planners study them to make predictions and plan for the future. Companies use the data to decide what to make and sell—and where.

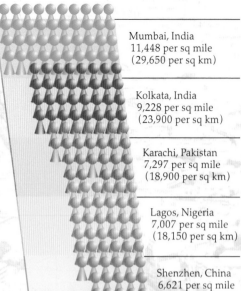

Mumbai, India
11,448 per sq mile
(29,650 per sq km)

Kolkata, India
9,228 per sq mile
(23,900 per sq km)

Karachi, Pakistan
7,297 per sq mile
(18,900 per sq km)

Lagos, Nigeria
7,007 per sq mile
(18,150 per sq km)

Shenzhen, China
6,621 per sq mile
(17,150 per sq km)

Population density, people per square mile (kilometer), in 2007

THE POPULATION CRUNCH
Population density is the number of people occupying a certain area of land, such as a square mile. Various factors make for crowded cities. Island cities such as Lagos may have no room to spread out. However, the most important factor is rapid, uncontrolled urbanization—the movement of rural people into cities in search of a better income. New arrivals who are too poor to afford proper housing are forced to crowd into dense slums, as in Mumbai or Karachi.

THE HIGHEST OF THE HIGH
The skyscraper revolution began in the US, but today the tallest towers are mainly in Asian cities. Most have been built in the past 10 years. The pictures below show buildings in order of roof or spire height, but not antenna height. This is why the Petronas Towers are taller than the Willis Tower. Missing from this list is New York City's World Trade Center, whose twin towers rose to 1,368 ft (417 m) and 1,362 ft (415 m). When built in 1972, they were the world's tallest buildings, but they were destroyed in a terrorist attack in 2001.

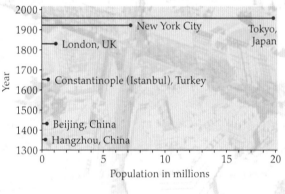

Year / Population in millions

New York City — Tokyo, Japan
London, UK
Constantinople (Istanbul), Turkey
Beijing, China
Hangzhou, China

HISTORICAL EXPANSION
This chart shows at which point in history a city became the biggest in the world, and what its population was at that time. Such statistics help us to understand the economic and political forces that affect the rise and fall of certain cities. Factors such as trade, industry, migration, invasion, disease, and changing climate affect the growth of cities. London's rise to biggest-city status coincided with urbanization caused by the Industrial Revolution.

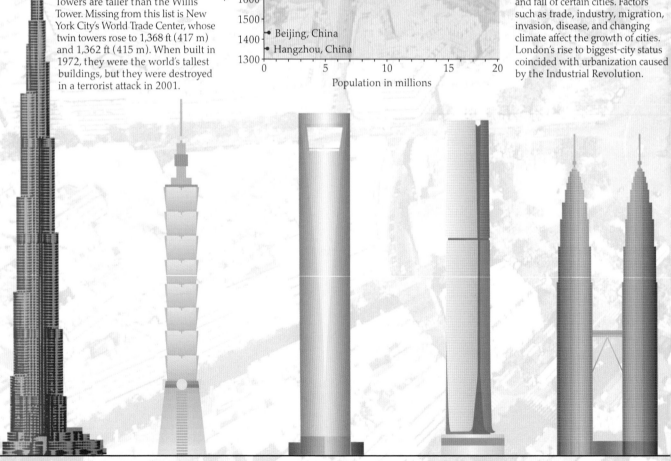

Burj Khalifa, Dubai, UAE
Built 2010,
2,717 ft (828 m)

Taipei 101, Taipei, Taiwan
Built 2004,
1,671 ft (509 m)

Shanghai World Financial
Center, Shanghai, China
Built 2008, 1,614 ft (492 m)

International Commerce
Center, Hong Kong, China
Built 2010, 1,588 ft (484 m)

Petronas Towers,
Kuala Lumpur, Malaysia
Built 1998, 1,483 ft (452 m)

MOST VISITED CITIES

This map shows cities with the largest number of arrivals between 2006 and 2008. London, UK, drew the largest number of international visitors due to its combined attraction as a business and tourist destination. Antalya, Turkey, is another popular destination, as its airport serves the entire tourism region of the Turkish Mediterranean coast.

New York City
24.7 million

Paris
35.8 million

London
43 million

Istanbul
13 million

Bangkok
31.4 million

Antalya
15.6 million

Dubai
20.2 million

Hong Kong
27.5 million

Kuala Lumpur
8.9 million

Singapore
29.9 million

New York, 3,352 sq miles (8,683 sq km)

Tokyo, 2,700 sq miles (6,993 sq km)

Chicago, 2,123 sq miles (5,498 sq km)

Atlanta, 1,962 sq miles (5,083 sq km)

Philadelphia, 1,800 sq miles (4,661 sq km)

METROPOLITAN SPRAWL

The cities shown here are the world's largest in area. The areas given include the surrounding continuous urban region of each city. With the exception of Tokyo, which in every way is the world's largest city, these are not the cities with the most people. They are the most spread-out cities—those with the most urban sprawl. Large, sprawling cities may offer cheaper land and quiet suburbs, but people have to travel great distances to their workplaces, stores, and schools, either in private cars or by public transportation. The residents of these cities have to consume a lot of fuel getting from place to place.

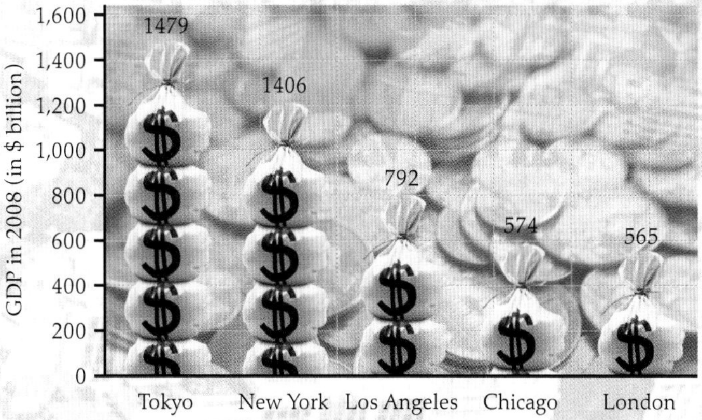

GDP in 2008 (in $ billion)

1479 — Tokyo
1406 — New York
792 — Los Angeles
574 — Chicago
565 — London

THE PRODUCERS OF WEALTH

A city's ability to create wealth is indicated by its Gross Domestic Product (GDP). This is the market value of all the goods and services produced in a city (or a country) over a year. It shows total economic output, so a bigger city is likely to have a larger GDP than a smaller one, regardless of whether its citizens are richer or not. Nevertheless, the world's top five wealth producers, shown here, are all big cities in rich countries.

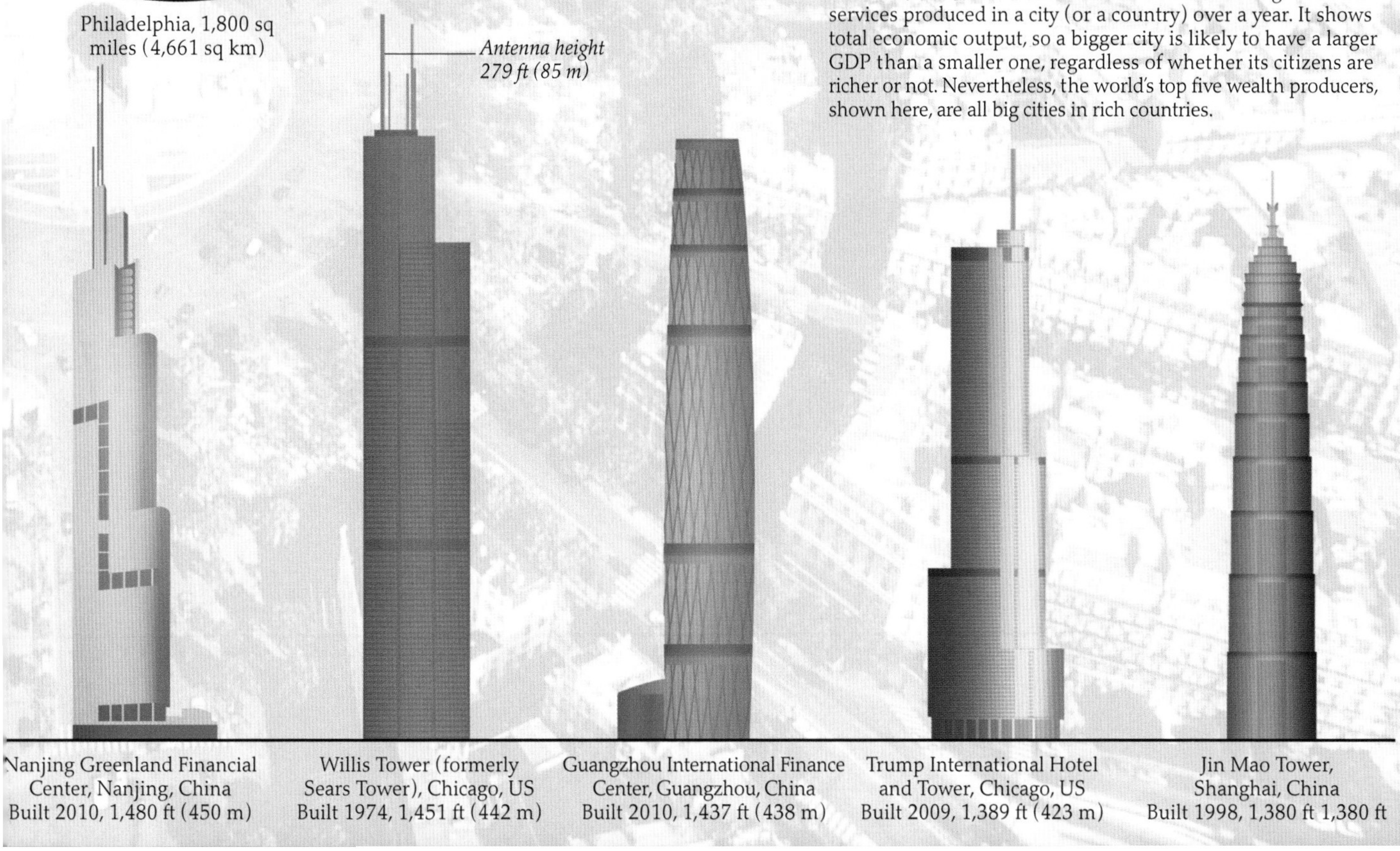

Antenna height 279 ft (85 m)

Nanjing Greenland Financial Center, Nanjing, China
Built 2010, 1,480 ft (450 m)

Willis Tower (formerly Sears Tower), Chicago, US
Built 1974, 1,451 ft (442 m)

Guangzhou International Finance Center, Guangzhou, China
Built 2010, 1,437 ft (438 m)

Trump International Hotel and Tower, Chicago, US
Built 2009, 1,389 ft (423 m)

Jin Mao Tower, Shanghai, China
Built 1998, 1,380 ft 1,380 ft

Glossary

Causeway connecting Singapore with Johor Bahru, Malaysia

AQUEDUCT
A channel or pipe carrying water, sometimes supported by a high bridge.

ARCHEOLOGIST
Someone who excavates and studies ancient sites and remains, methodically and scientifically.

ARCHITECTURE
1) The art and science of building.
2) The style in which buildings are designed.
3) A group of buildings and other large structures.

ASSEMBLY
A gathering of citizens or representatives.

AVENUE
A broad street lined with trees.

CAPITALISM
An economic system in which the means of production (such as factories and offices) are owned by individuals and not by the government.

CATACOMB
An underground cemetery with chambers for coffins or ossuaries (stores of bones).

CAUSEWAY
A raised path or road that crosses a marsh, shore, or seabed.

CCTV
Closed-circuit television—the recording of images by cameras set up in public places to monitor traffic, security, or crime.

CARNIVAL
A festival of merrymaking and parades, originally held annually before the Christian period of Lent.

CENSUS
The official counting of people living within a particular area, and the collection of data about them.

CITADEL
A fortified section within an ancient city, used for defense or control.

CITY
1) Any large or populous urban area.
2) The inner districts of a larger urban area.
3) An urban area with particular political, religious, or administrative status.

CITY-STATE
A city, such as Singapore, that rules itself and neighboring territory as a nation.

CIVILIZATION
A society that has developed arts, sciences, government, and the rule of law.

CIVIL SERVICE
The public servants and officials who organize and carry out acts of government.

CONURBATION
The merging of separate cities or urban areas as they grow larger. Also, the large, multicentered settlement that results from this merging.

COUNCIL
A group of elected officials who supervise the day-to-day running of a city or region.

CUNEIFORM
Wedge-shaped, describing a form of writing used in the first cities, in ancient Iraq.

CURFEW
A limit on the public movement of people at certain times of the day or night, in the interests of public order.

DEMOCRACY
A political system in which the citizens of the country choose, by voting, people to represent them in the government.

Grid pattern in the city of Talca, Chile

DESALINATION
The removal of salt from sea water, so that it can be used for drinking or farming.

DOWNTOWN
The central business district of a city.

ECONOMY
The system of money, exchange, business, trade, labor, and manufacture.

ETHNIC GROUP
Any group of people sharing the same ancestral background or cultural heritage.

FEDERAL
Belonging to a political organization of separate states, in which the members are partly independent, such as the US.

FINANCE
1) Money as a resource, funding, or revenue.
2) The business of banking or investment.

FOREIGN EXCHANGE
The buying and selling of international currencies.

FOUNDATIONS
The underground structures supporting a building.

A meeting of the City Municipal Council in Marseille, France

GDP
Gross Domestic Product—a measure of wealth creation. It represents the total value of goods and services produced within a city or a nation over a given period.

GRAFFITI
Words or images scratched or painted in public places, often on walls, bridges, or subway cars.

GREEN BELT
Areas of grassland or woodland that are preserved by law and not built upon.

GRID PATTERN
City street layout based on straight roads and rectangular blocks of buildings.

HIGH-RISE
Having many stories, as a tall apartment building or a skyscraper.

HINTERLAND
1) An inland area supplying goods to a port.
2) Any region upon which a city depends for its supplies.

INDUSTRIAL REVOLUTION
A period of change brought about in the 1700s and 1800s by the invention of machines that allowed goods to be mass produced in factories. Thousands of factory laborers came to live in the first industrial towns.

INFRASTRUCTURE
The facilities and services that help a city to function, such as transportation, electricity, water supply and drainage, and communication networks.

LANDMARK
A prominent monument, building, or natural feature.

MANUFACTURE
The making of goods by hand or by machine.

MEGA-REGION
A vast urban area—a conurbation of conurbations.

MEGACITY
Any city that has spread to create a huge urban area.

METROPOLIS
1) The mother city of a colonial settlement in ancient Greece. 2) The chief city in a nation or region, not necessarily the capital. 3) The greater area of a city, including central and outlying areas.

MIGRATION
A movement of people from one region or country to another.

MINARET
The high tower of a mosque.

Spire of Chichester Cathedral, UK

PARKOUR
An athletic, but noncompetitive sport based on adapting the urban environment as an obstacle course. Closely related to freerunning.

PILE
A long pillar of timber, concrete, or metal driven deep into the ground as a foundation for a building.

PILGRIMAGE
A journey made to a religious shrine or site, for reasons of faith.

POLLUTION
The poisoning of air, land, or water by domestic or industrial waste, or gas emissions.

POPULATION
The number of people living within a particular area.

RADIOACTIVE
Giving out radiation as a result of changes in a substance's atomic structure.

RAMPARTS
Outer fortifications—usually an earth embankment but may include stone walls.

RECYCLE
To reuse materials such as paper, cloth, wood, glass, metal, or plastic in order to avoid waste, save resources, and make new products.

REGENERATION
Giving new life to a run-down urban area by redesigning buildings, providing better facilities, and finding ways to gain investors' money and provide jobs to the residents.

RURAL
To do with, or living in, the countryside.

SATELLITE TOWN
A town outside the city limits, but depending on that city for work or resources.

SERVICE INDUSTRY
An industry that provides services rather than products, such as transportation, tourism, or insurance.

SEWER
A pipe, tunnel, or channel that takes away domestic or industrial waste and drainage water from a city.

SHANTY TOWN
A district of temporary, makeshift shacks and slums often built illegally. Known as favelas in Brazil.

Ramparts of Carcassonne, France

SIEGE
A military tactic in which the attacking army cuts off a city's supplies to force it to surrender.

SKYSCRAPER
A very tall building with many stories.

SLUM
Run-down housing with poor facilities.

SPIRE
A tall, pointed pinnacle rising from the roof of a building, especially a church.

STOCK EXCHANGE
A place where people buy and sell shares of a company. A share is a certificate of part-ownership of a company.

SUBURB
1) In the UK and Ireland, any residential areas outside the inner districts of a city.
2) In North America, an outlying town or residential area not included within the city administration.
3) In Australia and New Zealand, geographical subdivisions of the city administration.

TERRORIST
Any government, organization, or individual seeking to achieve political change by striking fear into people, often through violence.

URBAN
To do with, or living in, a town or city.

URBAN DECAY
The decline of certain city districts due to economic or social changes, such as relocation of key industries to other areas, leading to unemployment and poverty.

URBAN SPRAWL
The outward spread of a city into suburban and rural areas.

VANDALISM
Any deliberate act designed to destroy or spoil the appearance of public or private property.

ZIGGURAT
A large temple mound built in the ancient cities of the Middle East.

Index

Acknowledgments

Dorling Kindersley would like to thank:
Caitlin Doyle for proofreading and Jackie Brind for the index.

The publishers would like to thank the following for their kind permission to reproduce their photographs:

(Key: a-above; b/g-background; b-below/bottom; bl-below left; br-below right; c-center; cl-center left; cr-center right; l-left; r-right; t-top, tl-top left; tr-top right; crb-center right below; cra-center right above.)

akg-images: John Hios 44tl. Alamy Images: An Qi 51b; Krys Bailey 2cl, 54tl; E.J. Baumeister Jr 25c; Eric Brown 61tr; Rob Crandall 45br; Eastland Photo 7tr; EmmePi Images 58cra; Tony Eveling 56clb; Colin Galloway 59tr; Peter Horree 20cr; imagebroker 9c; Stuart Jenner 62cl; JTB Photo Communications, Inc. 55tl; Linda Kennedy 71b; Mary Evans Picture Library 21tl, 60tl; Steven May 45cr; Eric Nathan 41cl; Niday Picture Library 20b; North Wind Picture Archives 26tl; Photos 12 37tl, 38cl; Picture Contact 31tl; Leonid Plotkin 59br; qaphotos.com 41br; Robert Harding Picture Library Ltd 2tr, 38bl; Friedrich Stark 25crb; Zhu Tianchun/TAO Images Limited 48-49; Stacy Walsh Rosenstock 1tl. ARCADD, Inc.: Dr. Hisham N. Ashkouri, AIA 27crb; . Photography © The Art Institute of Chicago: Edward Hopper, American, 1882-1967, Nighthawks, 1942, Oil on canvas, 84.1 x 152.4 cm (33 1/8 x 60 in.) Friends of American Art Collection, 1942.51, The Art Institute of Chicago. 56tl. The Art Archive: Bibliothèque Nationale Paris 22cl; Arte Primitivo 4cl, 9cl; Gianni Dagli Orti/Museo del Templo Mayor Mexico 40c; Museo Nazionale Taranto/Alfredo Dagli Orti 50tl. Bruce Moffat Collection: 41tr. Corbis: David Arky 2br,

37br; Yann Arthus-Bertrand 64-65 (Background), 66-67 (Background), 70-71 (Background); Yann Arthus-Bertrand / Jean-François Chalgrin 26b; Atlantide Phototravel 42cl; B.S.P.I. 4crb, 62tr; Gaetan Bally/ Keystone 7tl; Bettmann 22-23c (air raid), 29cra, 42bc, 60-61 (Background); Walter Bibikow / JAI 39tr; Bilderbuch/ Design Pics 67cb; Sébastien Cailleux 12-13tc; Stéphane Cardinale / Sygma 57cra; John Carnemolla 38-39br; Alan Copson/ JAI 43tr; P. Deliss / Godong 4tl, 12tl; Patrick Escudero/ Hemis 67tl; Michele Falzone/JAI 13cr, 27tr; Bertrand Gardel/ Hemis 67cdb; Lowell Georgia 67tr; Justin Guariglia 47cra; Halaska, Jacob/ Index Stock 50bl; Paul Hardy 36tl; Angelo Hornak 48tl; K. J. Historical 16c; Wolfgang Kaehler 66br; Mike Kemp/In Pictures 57tl; Bob Krist 69cb; James Leynse 43crb; Josef Lindau 53b; John Lund/Paula Zacharias/Blend Images 62cr; Mark Mawson Robert Harding World Imagery 7tr; David Mercado/Reuters 59cla; moodboard 35cra; Sergio Moraes/Reuters 54b; Larry Mulvehill 30-31b; Ocean 51tr; Gianni Dagli Orti 9tr; Alberto Pizzoli/ Sygma 58-59 (Background); Michael Prince 6-7b; José Fuste Raga 18bl; Bertrand Rieger/ Hemis 40crb; Tony Savino 50cb; Phil Schermeister 25tl; Schlegelmilch 53tl; Paul Seheult/Eye Ubiquitous 66cla; Bill Stormont 45tl; E. Streichan 66ca; Ted Spiegel 20cla, 20tl; Nico Tondini /Robert Harding World Imagery 18c; David Turnley 23c; Jean-Michel Turpin 31cl; John Van Hasselt 52cr; Isabelle Vayron/Sygma 16tl; David Vintiner 67tr; WWD/Condé Nast 36bl; Michael Yamashita 49bl, 64bl. Dorling Kindersley: ARF/TAP (Archaeological Receipts Fund) 66clb; Arte Primitivo 4cl, 9cl; Courtesy of Patrice Reboul 22bc; Courtesy of the Museo Archeologico Nazionale di Napoli 16clb; Courtesy of the University Museum of Archaeology and Anthropology, Cambridge 9cr; Exeter City Museums and Art Gallery, Royal Albert Memorial Museum 22br; Rough Guides 70tc; Michel Zabe/ Conaculta-Inah-Mex 3tl, 52tl. Flickr.com: Joerg Zwingli 46bl. fotolia: Natalia Bratslavsky 67cra;

Comugnero Silvana 3tr, 44clb. Frederick Warne & Co.,: Cover of The Tale of Johnny Town-Mouse by Beatrix Potter/ Reproduced by permission of Frederick Warne & Co./ 1918 7cr. Getty Images: 29br, 55tr, 60c, 67bl; AFP 11tl, 28cr, 32b, 33tr, 35bl, 52bl, 54tr, 55br, 61crb, 66bc, 70bl; Altrendo Travel 2cr, 9br; Colin Anderson 64br; Antoine Antoniol / Bloomberg 49tl; John W Banagan 15tl; Nathan Blaney / Flickr 3b, 26-27 (road intersection); Ira Block 8b; Bloomberg 21br, 21tr, 65cl; Tom Bonaventure 64tl; Brand X Pictures 21cl; Buena Vista Images 69cla; Paul Chesley 32cl; Max Dannenbaum / The Image Bank 12-13b; Bruno De Hogues 35crb; DEA Picture Library 60cl; Sam Diephuis 6cla; Sally Dillon 65br; Jerry Driendl 69cl (Atlanta); Andre Gallant 59tl; Hisham Ibrahim 64cra; Image Source 69cr (Money bags); John Lamb 67cr; LatinContent 52c; Siegfried Layda 4b, 28-29 (Skyscrapers); Peter Macdiarmid 35tr; Diane Macdonald 69cr; David McNew 34-35tc; Ryan McVay 69tr (Red luggage); Medioimages / Photodisc 27ca; Toshitaka Morita 6tl; Sarah Murray 66bl; Narinder Nanu / AFP 13tr; Kazuhiro Nogi / AFP 23tr; Nomadic Luxury 69cl (Tokyo); Planet Observer / Universal Images Group 62clb; PNC 50cra; Ingolf Pompe / LOOK-foto 64clb; R H Productions 69cl (Chicago); RedChopsticks 8tl; Stuart Redler 42-43c; Adalberto Rios Szalay / Sexto Sol 65cr; Alessandro Rizzi 37tr; Sabine Scheckel 4tr, 25tr; Tom Stoddart 19bc; Luca Tettoni 5tr, 47cl; The Bridgeman Art Library 14c; Alan Traeger 30cra; Travel Ink 42tl; Guy Vanderelst 66tl; Susan Watts / NY Daily News Archive 39tl; Win Initiative 70cr; Alison Wright/ Robert Harding 14bl. iStockphoto. com: Efesan 1c, 46-47c; Inna Felker 1l, 46ccb; Jonathan Maddock 16bc; Rasmushald 1r, 47bl; Anthony Rosenberg 64crb; shishic 15b. Joel Gordon Photography: 34crb. Yves Marchand & Romain Meffre: 33cra. Govind Mittal: 24tl. MVRDV: 63b. NASA: GSFC/METI/ERSDAC/ JAROS, and U.S./Japan ASTER Science Team 17tl. naturepl.com: Laurent Geslin 49crcb. Joe Nishizawa:

Metropolitan Area Outer Underground Discharge Channel 41tl. Photolibrary: 10-11b; Bartomeu Amengual / age fotostock 57br; W Buss 37b; Robert Clark / Aurora Photos 23br; Günter Flegar 14tl; Godong 33tl; Hiroshi Higuchi 6cl; imagebroker.net 37cr; Japan Travel Bureau / Haga Library 12cb; Kordcom 15tr; V Muthuraman 62br; Pixtal Images 24b; Alexis Platoff 11cr; Erwan Quemere 19t; Guido Alberto Rossi 10tl; The Print Collector 7cl; Paul Underhill / PYMCA 56-57c; Ivan Vdovin 67cla; Steve Vidler 11cr. Photoshot: UPPA 44-45bc. Press Association Images: Jin Lee / AP 36-37c. Reuters: Romeo Ranoco 32tl. The Ronald Grant Archive: 20th Century Fox 17tr. TfL from the London Transport Museum collection: 30tl. TopFoto. co.uk: The Granger Collection 63tc. U.S. Geological Survey: Ron Beck, USGS Eros Data Center Satellite Systems Branch 31tr. University of Chicago: Oriental Institute, Hamoukar Expedition 9cla.

Jacket: Front: Getty Images: Fuse b. Back: Corbis: B.S.P.I. cla; Ocean tl; fotolia: Comugnero Silvana tr; Getty Images: Luca Tettoni cb; Alison Wright / Robert Harding bl; iStockphoto.com: Efesan c; Inna Felker c; Rasmushald c; TfL from the London Transport Museum collection: crb.

Wall chart: Alamy Images: Krys Bailey fcr; imagebroker cla; Corbis: Atlantide Phototravel clb (cistern); B.S.P.I. crb (car); Michael Prince b; Tony Savino cr; David Turnley cr (soldiers); Dorling Kindersley: Courtesy of the Museo Archeologico Nazionale di Napoli cla (plaster cast); Getty Images: John W Banagan tl (pagoda); Nathan Blaney / Flickr cla (signs); LatinContent bl; Stuart Redler bl; Govind Mittal: ca; Photoshot: UPPA cb; Press Association Images: Jin Lee / AP tr.

All other images © Dorling Kindersley
For further information see: www.dkimages.com